HENDERSON'S LIGHT

"Drinking, driving and a deadly encounter"

by Jack Torry

HENDERSON'S LIGHT

"Drinking, driving and a deadly encounter"

by Jack Torry

Countinghouse Press, Inc.

Bloomfield Hills, Michigan

HENDERSON'S LIGHT

First Edition

ISBN-13: 978-0-9786191-9-0
ISBN-10: 0-9786191-9-6

Printed in the United States of America by
Cover design by Sans Serif, Saline, Michigan

Front cover image of the Buick involved in the 1965 crash is reproduced courtesy of the Birmingham, Michigan Historical Museum and Park Archives.

For Pam, David and Matt

CONTENTS

INTRODUCTION

As she stood in line listening to the sounds of laughter and reunion gossip, she wasn't sure she belonged with the 150 people making their way into an elegant ballroom in suburban Detroit. After all, those who gathered to celebrate their 40th high school re-union had been part of her older brother's class, not hers. And Roddy had been gone for so long, she doubted they would remember him, much less recognize her. Then she spied a hallway table neatly lined with rows of nametags. One read: "Nancy Henderson." Underneath in parenthesis it said: "Roddy's sister."

All this cool summer day in 2006 she had been thinking of Roddy and the people he knew so well. There was Peachie, the petite blonde with the vibrant laugh; Sandy, the tall tomboy who loved to swim and play baseball, and wasn't afraid to take on the boys; Mike, so short his friends called him Mouse; Bruce, the shy boy with the light blue eyes and blond hair. And Roddy, the special one with the zesty smile–the championship swimmer who surely would have been a star on the U.S. Olympic team, the dazzling brother she adored but never felt equal to.

In the late afternoon, she walked about the basin near the private school at Cranbrook where as a kid Roddy recklessly raced his bike against the sloped banks–playing hard and showing off, as always. She stopped by the sandstone church in Bloomfield Hills where on a snowy afternoon so many years ago, they held a memorial service for the kids. Then east on Maple Road toward uptown Birmingham and the sloping curve between Lake Park and Aspen streets, just west of the waterfall that empties Quarton Lake. Just about every time she drove past the curve she thought about the convertible with long-necked beer bottles in the back seat, the convertible that slammed into Roddy's Buick. This was the curve where Roddy and two friends died, and where two others were left battered and unconscious.

Everything there looked exactly as it did in 1965 with one glaring exception: After the crash, city officials installed a traffic light at the corner of Lake Park and Maple. They hoped it would force drivers to slow down as they reached the curve in the road. Henderson's Light, some of Roddy's buddies called it. It marked a crash that rocked an upper middle class community and inflicted deep emotional scars on so many. It was the spot where Nancy's childhood came to an abrupt end at the age of 13.

She attached her nametag to the lapel of her dusty-pink jacket and walked into the ballroom. To her astonishment, Roddy's old friends engulfed her. They laughed about the time Roddy played a beatnik in an elementary school play and horrified his teachers by clutching an unlit cigarette as he bounded about the stage. She lost count of the number of women in their late 50s who revealed their intense crushes on Roddy in school. One of Roddy's friends brought a grade-school class photo where you could make out a serious-looking Sandy, and a grinning Mike. Just behind them was Roddy, wearing a plaid shirt and, ever the class clown, pretending to strangle the girl in front of him. Another woman produced tiny black-and-white Polaroid photos of Peachie, her face accentuated by her trademark smile. Did she ever frown? "You know, Roddy and Peachie are here tonight, just loving it," somebody said with a laugh.

Nancy saw Mike. He was heavier and a bit grayer than she recalled from school. Anyone looking at Mike that night would never have known he had nearly died in a car crash. But Nancy knew better. There had been five major operations. A bit of Dacron held his aorta together. A stainless steel screen concealed a hole in his forehead. Mike was happy to see Nancy; he had helped arrange her invitation. They laughed as friends snapped photographs with their digital cameras. Then they talked by cell phone with Bruce from his home in Massachusetts. They so much wanted Bruce to be there. But Bruce, a veterinarian, could not get away for the weekend from the clinic he owns in Duxbury.

Since the night that Roddy and his friends died, half-a-million people have been killed in alcohol-related crashes in the United States. This is the story of just one of those crashes. It took place in the Detroit suburbs on a bitterly cold January night in 1965, but it could have happened during Christmas of 2007 in Ohio when a drunken man rammed his pickup truck into a minivan, killing five people. It could have been in March of 2009 in another Detroit suburb when a 47-year-old woman who was legally drunk smashed her Ford van into a red Chevrolet Cobalt, killing four teenagers who were on their way to pick up a pizza. Or it could have been April of 2009 near Anaheim, California, when a 22-year-old man whose license had been suspended because of a drunk driving conviction ran through a red light and slammed his van into a silver Mitsubishi Eclipse, killing 22-year-old Los Angeles Angels pitcher Nick Adenhart and two of his friends. Much like the aftermath of every crash involving drinking, it is a narrative of hidden fears and misplaced guilt, of alcoholism and early deaths of grieving relatives, and wounds that never quite heal. And it is a tenacious four-decade struggle for recovery by three teenagers and a 10 year old girl, who the moment before the collision, seemed to have everything in their lives.

PROLOGUE

The young driver with slicked back brown hair and the look of the Fonz pressed down on the accelerator until his 1955 Chevy reached 90 miles an hour, roaring past a small drug store on the left and a church of Tudor design on the right. He and a close friend riding shotgun had been to a hockey game. Now they were capping off the evening by downing a few beers and racing about the streets of suburban Detroit. As the Chevy careened toward uptown Birmingham, a collection of fashionable boutiques and trendy restaurants, the young driver reached a bend in the road. He missed the turn and knocked down a utility pole, dragging it more than 150 feet before car and pole slammed into a second utility pole.

Within minutes of the 4 a.m. crash that December morning in 1961, Patrolmen Harold Jones and Charles Blashfield arrived to find the driver pinned under the car. Jones fished out a jack, attached it to the front bumper and the two officers raised the car and tugged the driver free. The young man was chattering away, asking over and over where his friend was. The puzzled officers searched about until they found the second boy about 100 feet away. Both boys miraculously had survived.

Three years later, Officer Jones was summoned to another accident involving the same young man at the same bend in the road. On this Saturday night, the young man raced at more than 70 miles per hour in his black Ford Galaxie convertible powered by a Thunderbird 390 engine with white-wall tires and bulleted front grill. In the back seat, he had two cases of long-necked beer bottles of Pabst Blue Ribbon and six steaks he bought just a few hours earlier. As he approached the same bend he missed in 1961, the driver once again darted across the dividing line. This time, instead of hitting a telephone pole, he smashed into a burgundy Buick Skylark filled with five teenagers who had been out for pizza and coke. The collision hurtled the Skylark back more than 60 feet until it slammed into a third car. Twisted scraps of metal and a 16-year-old boy's wristwatch littered the cement pavement. The police towed the battered hulks to gas station lots in Birmingham where I first saw them as a 13-year-old junior high school student. I did not know the kids, but throughout the years when I would read about a drunk-driving crash, I thought of those two wrecked cars. Who were these kids who died? What happened to the survivors? Four decades after the crash, I decided to find out.

What I learned was this crash was no fleeting event, but instead a wound seared into the memories of everyone involved. I suspected it was the same as tens of thousands of other alcohol-related accidents that occur with mind-numbing regularity. The reader of this book has about a 40 percent chance in his or her lifetime of being involved in a crash involving alcohol. The leading cause of death in America for those between ages four and 34 is an automobile accident. Yet these cold statistics are, in the words of one expert, largely ignored by public officials and news organizations. "Gruesome crashes are reported just one at a time, each as if it might never happen again," Peter J. Wooley, a professor of political science at Farleigh Dickinson University wrote in 2006 in the *Washington Post*.

I also found out something else: Like all crashes involving alcohol, what happened was not fate or bad luck, but bad judgment by one young man. Well-liked by his friends as a high school student in Pittsburgh, he did not have a reputation as a troublemaker. But that night, he scarred the lives of people he never knew. For those in the Skylark and Galaxie, as well as everyone close to them, life as they knew it ended that night.

ONE

"Mr. Cool"

They were the elite of high school swimming in Michigan. Eighteen swimmers and divers from the two schools would qualify for the state championship meet in March at Michigan State University. A dozen would make high school all-American. Four would make the finals of the 100-yard freestyle at the state meet. Two were future state champions. And there was one, a junior, who just about everyone thought would be a member of the U.S. Olympic team someday.

On this gray, frigid afternoon, so typical for January in the Detroit suburbs, Battle Creek Central and Birmingham Seaholm would engage in yet another warm-up for the state meet. They had competed against one another in relays a month earlier in Battle Creek, a meet that attracted the finest of Michigan's swimmers. Seaholm handily won that encounter and was expected to win again in a dual meet at Seaholm's new pool. With its six lanes and twin one-meter diving boards illuminated by overhead lights, the pool was one of the showplaces for high school swimming. Central was good, a school that had won 15 state championships since 1931. But by 1965, Seaholm had eclipsed Central, winning or sharing the past three state titles and prevailing in 48 consecutive dual meets. Some Seaholm swimmers had never lost a meet in high school or junior high. They had a swagger that bordered on arrogance. Whenever they swam at another school, Seaholm's swimmers would bring along a jug of water from their own pool. Then, as they chanted their team nickname, "Maples, Maples," they smugly poured the water into the home team's pool.

Seaholm's fastest swimmer was Roddy Henderson, a freestyler equally adept at butterfly and backstroke. Corey Van Fleet, who directed the Seaholm team, thought Henderson was a swimmer of "national caliber" and was certain he would be an NCAA champion. Friends urged Roddy to swim at Michigan State University, but coaches from such fabled programs as Indiana University were hoping to lure him to their schools. Just the previous week, the Detroit News had showcased Roddy by publishing a photo of him poised to leap into the pool.

He had the consummate blend of good looks, athletic skill and audacity, giving everyone the impression he relished every moment in his life. He was a superlative swimmer without trying very hard. He was confident, even cocky. He never agonized over a rare loss. He earned good grades without applying himself. He rode horses and loved to be photographed in a cowboy hat and boots while twirling a rope. He admired James Dean and displayed a poster of the iconoclastic actor in his bedroom. He wrote witty lyrics, read Tennyson, played bongo drums and sang Calypso solos in school shows. Every boy envied him and every girl wanted to date him.

He had grown past six feet in height, but like many swimmers of the era was slender. With his lean build and lackadaisical style, he looked and swam like Gary Hall Jr., a two-time Olympian who would win four gold medals at the 1996 and 2000 summer games. As Roddy added weight and became stronger, there was every reason to believe his times would plummet. Van Fleet recognized that at age 16, Roddy still was just a "kid who swam fast" rather than a polished swimmer who trained hard all year. Van Fleet thought he had the "reactions of a cat," allowing him to get a swift start off the blocks, a crucial requirement in races as short as the 100 freestyle. Before each race, a nonchalant Roddy stood on the block completely at ease, giving everyone the impression that he could not care less about the upcoming event. But as the starter fired the pistol, Roddy exploded into the water, far ahead of competitors. He almost always stayed ahead of them. (1)

Teammates marveled at Roddy's effortless speed. During practice others would watch Roddy "fool around" and "count the squares on the bottom" of the pool. Bored by workouts, Roddy amused himself by playing jacks on the pool deck; the student newspaper proclaimed him the team's jacks' champion. "We were probably a little jealous because it looked so easy for him," said one teammate. To push him,

Van Fleet devised ingenious gimmicks. Toward the end of a long workout, he would strike a deal with Roddy: Swim a fast time in the 100, and in return, the team could go home early. Properly motivated and urged on by his cheering teammates, Roddy would burst from the blocks and beat any time Van Fleet prescribed. (2)

Yet despite Roddy's apparent disdain for hard work, he already was the premier sprinter in Michigan, a state that perpetually produced waves of outstanding swimmers. He liked the shorter events, figuring that he earned the same number of points for winning a sprint as for winning a longer, more demanding event. (3) As a sophomore at the 1964 state championship, Roddy finished third in the 100-yard freestyle and earned all-American honors by anchoring Seaholm's 200-yard freestyle relay. Now as a junior, he had the second fastest time in Michigan in the 100 and there was every reason to believe that by year's end he would be closing in on Olympian Don Schollander's national high school record. Roddy ranked fifth in Michigan in both the 50 and 200 freestyle. During the 200-yard medley relay one month earlier at the Battle Creek team relays, Roddy anchored the final leg as Seaholm set a pool record. Just two weeks earlier, he had been the No. 1 junior at the 16-team Ann Arbor relays. Roddy, said one teammate, "was a natural."

A week before the Central High School meet, Roddy was weak from the flu, a virus that customarily played havoc with Midwest teams during January and February. But knowing the meet would be close, Van Fleet wanted Roddy to swim, telling a reporter that "you don't leave your big man out of a key meet if he can get you any points at all." (4) A typically large and raucous Seaholm crowd of more than a thousand gathered, including Roddy's girlfriend – he always seemed to have one – Barbara Barnum, a petite 16-year-old blonde with an infectious laugh and the nickname Peachie, which most shortened to Peach. She sat with her closest friend, Sandy Christman, a 17-year-old junior just back from scuba diving in sunny Mexico. After the meet, Peachie and Sandy planned to join Roddy and teammates Mike Adair and Bruce Berridge for a pizza at one of

9

their favorite hangouts. Roddy would drive his mother's Buick Skylark.

His real name was Roger, but nobody ever called him that, preferring Rod or Roddy. His father Ed and mother Helen dubbed him Roddy from birth after they noticed friends using that nickname for their son Roger. Their choice produced endless confusion, with newspapers often spelling his name "Rodger." (5)

As a young boy, he was energetic and so constantly in motion that his mother thought of him as a troublemaker. At age three, he figured out a way to get the front door open and dash across the street before Helen realized he was out of the house. When his first-grade teacher punished him by making him sit in the hallway, a rebellious Roddy simply got up, left school and walked the five blocks home. When he was 13, Roddy, Mike and Bruce disappeared for several hours on their bikes to see Mike's girlfriend. When Roddy told his horrified mother that they had ridden to the next suburb, an exasperated Helen scolded him, "Roddy, next time you want to go somewhere, just tell me which direction you're going – north, east, south or west -- so I have an idea where to look for you." (6)

In a family of introverts, Roddy stood out, the one who shook things up. His younger sister Nancy thought of him as rebellious, always in search of the unusual. When Roddy wanted a pet, he selected a blue parakeet, named it Quito and taught him how to talk –Roddy's way. Friends entering the kitchen where the parakeet was housed in a cage would be greeted with a screech of, "Gimme a kiss," followed by a loud smooching sound, and, "My name is Key-toe." Roddy stuck his mouth up to the cage to teach Quito how to kiss and talk. (7)

He was, in the words of one friend, "game to do anything." In an elementary school play, Roddy played a beatnik, complete with black slacks and shirt, and a bongo drum. He was supposed to enter the stage snapping his fingers and saying, "Yeah man," but at the last moment he added a distinctive touch by sticking a cigarette in his mouth. The kids loved the act, but the teacher in charge of the production was appalled. The only thing that saved Roddy from discipline was that he had enough sense not to light the cigarette.

When Dave Nelson moved from California to Birmingham in the early 1960s, he taught Roddy the West Coast rage of skateboarding, which Birmingham kids called bun boarding because you always fell on your buns. Roddy and Dave found a steep hill near the Cranbrook private school and raced down the slope, occasionally trying to perform Figure-Eights around each other. They spoke of trying to dash down the hill while standing on their heads. Nelson also introduced Roddy to surfing, although without an ocean nearby, they had to improvise. Once in the late fall as the temperature plunged into the 30s, Roddy, Nelson and another friend drove across the Blue Water Bridge into Canada and dragged two of Nelson's surf boards to Lake Huron. Wearing bathing trunks, they leaped into the heavy surf and raced toward shore. After every trip, they dashed into the car to warm up. Then back to the waves. (8)

Roddy seemed the opposite of his brother Jim, who was three years older. Jim spent his summers at Culver Military Academy in Indiana where he liked the intense regimentation and scored high honors. By contrast, Roddy resisted anything so orderly, making it clear he had no interest in Culver. When his parents sent Roddy to Camp Nissokone, a YMCA camp on Lake Van Otten just above the state's thumb, he hated it. He badgered his parents with phone calls every night, claiming that he did not even have bed sheets, an assertion Helen found amusing because she personally had packed his sheets. Three weeks later, he was back home. (9)

He had a mischievous side, the wise guy poking fun at friends and adults. When the girls' eighth-grade water ballet team posed for its team picture, Roddy impulsively jumped into the photo, the only boy among 23 girls. Bored in class on a warm spring afternoon, he amused himself by sailing dozens of paper airplanes out the open window, earning the wrath of his teacher and a trip to the principal's office. In the ninth grade as the girls borrowed the boys' locker room to change for a water ballet meet, Roddy and a buddy boldly marched through the door, startling the girls who were putting on

11

their bathing suits. Back to the principal's office again. Before every meet, Van Fleet forced his swimmers to chug a nutriment milk shake that he thought would give them a burst of energy. Most swimmers detested the taste and envied the lucky divers who were allowed to skip the canned shake. Not content to simply complain, Roddy went one step further and authored a poem for his 10th grade English class:

> Twas the night before the meet, and all through my brain,
> Were hopes that, that night, Kimball's team would be slain.
> Our sweats were all hung in the lockers with care,
> In hopes a victorious team would be there.
> My teammates were resting on the locker room floor,
> Hoping for victory more and more;
> And I in my Speedo, and Corey in his ducks,
> Knew what we needed was a whole lot of luck;
> When out at the pool there arose such a clatter,
> I jumped from the floor to see what was the matter.
> Out to the pool deck I flew like a flash,
> Tore open the door, and out in a dash;
> When what to my wondering eyes should appear?
> But the whole Kimball team reacting from beer.
> The whole Kimball team was so plowed on their butts,
> I knew in a moment they had to be nuts.
> But wait! Then I saw! It wasn't really beer!
> It was something different, it did appear.
> All of a sudden, I caught a scent.
> It wasn't beer. It was Nutriment!
> The boys were so full of that awful brew,
> They were going crazy and their coach was too.(10)

His determination to do exactly as he pleased frustrated teachers and friends. He shrugged off Van Fleet's training rules that prohibited snow skiing during swimming season, although the combination of skiing and swimming made his legs sore. When a teacher assigned Roddy's class to research well-known poems about autumn, Roddy went his own way, too. He bought a spiral notebook and proceeded to copy 25 poems that had little to do with autumn, including "April Rain," by the 19th-century American poet Robert Loveman and Alfred Lord Tennyson's "Crossing the Bar." Unimpressed that Roddy had spent so much time digging through a wide variety of poems, the irritated teacher gave him a D+. "You failed to follow directions, namely keeping poems within the required categories," the teacher wrote. "Only 5 of your poems do such and even a couple of these caused one to stretch his imagination. You did a lovely job, and it's too bad such becomes useless due to your carelessness." (11)

As gifted as he was in the pool, Roddy was bored with swimming and hated Van Fleet's intense workouts. He told his mother he planned to quit the sport as a senior. He told friends that he had no intention of swimming in college, prompting one bemused friend to say, "No. You're too good." (12)

Roddy relished being the center of attention. When he was 12 years old, he was chosen by his choir teacher to sing a solo at a variety show put on by the sixth graders at Quarton Elementary School. The teacher had arranged for the students to perform songs from around the world, asking Roddy to sing "Matilda," the Calypso song made popular by Harry Belafonte. Roddy initially agreed, but as the date approached he balked at singing before his best friends and their parents. A couple of years earlier when Roddy sang a solo in a school play, some of the boys laughed. Afterward, Roddy was so hurt that he uncharacteristically cried. He didn't want to go through that again. You have a good voice, the teacher assured him. You'll do fine.

On the night of the show in the spring of 1960, a large crowd packed the school gymnasium and its balcony. Roddy donned white beachcombers, walked to the center of the elevated stage and sang lines from *Matilda*, a Caribbean song popularized by the singer Harry Belafonte. (13)

As Roddy finished, the crowd stood and cheered. He couldn't have been happier; he liked performing, and he loved music. He dabbled in one musical instrument after another. He banged on a set of drums in the basement, paddled bongos, and, to the astonishment of friends and family, took up the marimba, playing the song Nola. He borrowed sister Nancy's new guitar once, although to her intense annoyance he promptly broke one of the strings. He would retire to his second-floor bedroom, adorned with a large poster of James Dean and a Route 66 sign, and blast his favorite songs, including those by Ray Charles, to whom he took a particular liking. (14)

Like many American teens in mid-1960s, his taste in music was shifting from Bobby Vee, Frankie Avalon, Dion, Buddy Holly and Johnny Tillotson to the British rock groups elbowing American groups off the charts. When Ed Sullivan was about to introduce the Beatles to American TV audiences, Roddy excitedly telephoned Mike Adair and urged him to watch. That Sunday evening – February 9, 1964 –Roddy, Nancy and the rest of the Hendersons gathered in the living room. Standing before hundreds of screaming girls in the CBS auditorium in New York, Sullivan famously intoned, "Ladies and gentlemen, the Beatles." Then before an estimated 73 million viewers, Paul McCartney, John Lennon, Ringo Starr and George Harrison sang their most recognized hits, "I Want to Hold Your Hand," and "She Loves You." An excited Nancy decided, as most girls did, that Paul was the cutest. (15)

Roddy would tape record the latest rock songs on the radio, allowing him to save a few bucks on the 45-singles. He had plenty of AM stations to choose from. While parents preferred the sophisticated sound of J.P. McCarthy on WJR, kids flipped from WXYZ at 1270 to WKNR at 1310 to CKLW in Canada at 800. The trick was to change the stations so quickly that you did not miss the latest rock song. Roddy, in particular, liked the Beach Boys and yearned to surf in California. When Roddy and his friends got together, they would endlessly play the latest 45s until everyone agreed on the lyrics.

The revolution in music was transforming fashion as well. The wet-head was truly dead by 1964, as Roddy and other boys discarded hair cream and turned away from the Duck's Tail. They grew their hair longer and styled it in the surfer fashion introduced by the Beach Boys. This part of the fashion revolution did not always meet with the approval of Van Fleet, who demanded a shorter cut, once leaving a swimmer – and his Beatles' cut -- at home. Even a defiant personality like Roddy had to trim his hair during swim season. One Seaholm swimmer joked that Van Fleet cut his own hair every four days. This was the haircut of choice for his swimmers, too, which they disdainfully dubbed the "Corey Special." (16)

Girls absolutely adored Roddy. Partly, it was his charismatic personality—"the life of the party kind of guy," thought a Seaholm teammate. But girls also found him physically irresistible. He had light brown hair, greenish-brown eyes and "a smile that was ready to break out at any time." He opted for trendy thin ties, V-necked wool sweaters and narrow slacks, personally picking the latest styles from Hughes, Hatcher & Suffrin, an upscale men's store in the heart of uptown Birmingham. He ritually stood in front of the mirror on the door of the second-floor linen closet, tried on different clothes or tweaked his tie, sometimes striking a James Dean pose. He meticulously combed and brushed his hair until it looked just right. During the summer as he swam at Oakland Hills Country Club, he developed a deep tan. The sun bleached his hair into the sandy blond of a California surfer. "He knew he was cool," said Steve Matthews, who swam with Roddy at Oakland Hills. "He just had 'It.' And he knew he had 'It.' "(17)

Peachie Barnum was just the latest girl he took a liking to. He did not boast about the way girls found him attractive. Steve Matthews, who was two years younger, would press Roddy for details about his latest date. How far did he get with her, Matthews wanted to know? Roddy would respond with a half smile and a twinkle, but, to Matthews' intense disappointment, no details.

For three years in junior high, Roddy went steady with Anne Le Fevre. She was petite, flashed a zesty smile, and styled her dark brown hair short with bangs that nearly covered her right eye. She sang in the eighth-grade glee club, was selected as one of Barnum's eight cheerleaders in the ninth grade and performed for the Catalinas, the school's water ballet team. Anne was flirtatious, leaving one girl to mutter she was too much competition in the struggle for guys like Roddy. Like Roddy, she was rebellious, learning to smoke cigarettes at age 11.

She and Roddy would go steady, argue, break up, and go steady again. Anne thought he "was a hunk," and one of her close girlfriends teased her that she knew when she was thinking of Roddy because her face lit up with her "Roddy smile." (18) In turn, she mesmerized Roddy. When Anne took a turn modeling for a Birmingham store, Roddy and his friends were there for the show, although they could not resist some lighthearted teasing. Roddy was so impressed that in her eighth-grade yearbook he scribbled that he liked "the way you always act like a lady. That modeling school has done you good."

When they dated in junior high school, they needed rides from parents or older friends. Anne's father once drew the assignment of collecting the kids from a junior high play. To Anne's consternation, her friends grabbed the back seats of the maroon-and-white station wagon, forcing Anne to sit up front between Roddy and her father. Quickly showing he was not intimidated by the presence of Anne's father, Roddy startled her by slipping his left arm over her shoulder. In a light-hearted fashion, they talked about names they would like for their children, although they rarely could agree. Anne wanted a daughter named Gwen, but Roddy dismissed that, saying he preferred to name a boy after his older brother Jim.(19)

Despite their obvious attraction to each other, Roddy and Anne had a tempestuous relationship. When she showed interest in another guy in eighth grade, Roddy clearly was annoyed. A year later, his bewilderment in their relationship erupted in a long note he penned in her yearbook. With his knack for the distinctive, he wrote the note up the left-side margin, across the top, and then down the right side over 11 consecutive pages, scrupulously avoiding writing across any of the photos.

"Anne," he began, "Well, there's a lot I could say to you in this yearbook after the year that we've spent in the 9th grade. I could tell you how much I hate you or I could tell you how much I love you. I'm not sure which would be easier." Then Roddy went on to do both. "You do so many things to make me hate you and yet you do so many things to make me like you. You're so changeable," he wrote, adding two exclamation points. Turning the page, he continued, "Anyway, I can't sit here and tell you what a wonderful girl you are because . . . well, I just can't. If you sign my yearbook after you read this, you'll probably want to tell me off. But I guess I can't do anything about it now because I am writing in ink and I can't erase it. So I'd better stop here so I won't regret what I say. So, good luck, have fun, see 'ya next year, be good, and all that crap." He then scribbled, "Love 'ya, Roddy," thought better of it, and crossed out the words "love 'ya." Within minutes, Roddy regretted the note, explaining to one buddy that he just got carried away. (20)

In March of 1964, as she neared the end of her sophomore year at Seaholm, her father was transferred to Chicago and Anne moved away. She was crushed at leaving Birmingham, her close friends and, in particular, Roddy. He missed her, as well. He composed a sonnet, and while he did not address it to anyone, he apparently was thinking of Anne:

"The girl I love is pretty as can be,
So cute I have no power to resist,
Her body, which is wonderful to me
And when I hold her tight, I am in bliss.

I kiss her and my heart comes all aglow.
Her lips I know are oh so fine,
And when she holds me tight I always know,
She'll tell me that she loves me and she's mine.

Her beauty, which is so beyond compare,
Shines forth from her as man could never guess.
Her beauty is a thing that is so rare,
I love her more than words could e'er express.

I'll love this girl until our lives have passed,
And even after that, my love will last."(21)

To a handful of friends, Roddy seemed unusually unhappy after Anne moved, complaining to one that his sophomore year was "sort of wasted for me." He would meet a close friend in the school library and confide to her "about my problems," although he later told her he did not "want to bother you with my sorrows."(22) He told one former girlfriend that he was sure he would die young, perhaps like his idol James Dean. The girl laughed and told him to forget it. When Mike Adair heard, he dismissed it as Roddy's clever way to gain sympathy from some girl.(23) After all, Roddy often talked about having a big family with lots of boys. And nobody seemed to enjoy having fun more than he did.

Roddy was Corey Van Fleet's favorite. Van Fleet named his adopted son Rodney after his swimming star. At 29, Corey Van Fleet was the architect of the Seaholm dynasty and already one of the Midwest's premier young coaches. He was so youthful his swimmers addressed him as Corey rather than the more official "Coach." But such informality barely disguised his demanding style. He designed rigorous workouts at a time when swimming coaches were just beginning to link laborious training with ever-faster times. The long hours in the chlorine-filled pool produced burning eyes, sore shoulders and aching knees. The swimmers were convinced that Van Fleet saved his most grueling workouts for Fridays, figuring they would be too exhausted to stay out late that night. Behind his back, some of his swimmers called him Napoleon. One swimmer, who asked a girl to a Friday night movie, was so fatigued that he struggled to stay awake at the theater, prompting his worried date to wonder what was wrong with her. (24)

Van Fleet was a devotee of what coaches called interval training. Until the late 1950s, most coaches designed simple routines: Swim a few laps, kick a few laps, pull a few laps, and then swim 100 yards four times with a leisurely 10-minute break between each set. In a typical interval workout, Van Fleet would require his swimmers to do 10 sets of 100-yard sprints, providing a one-minute rest between each set. By March, the swimmer would only rest for 10 seconds between each set. To make certain every swimmer knew exactly when to start the new set, Van Fleet installed four large 60-second clocks at each corner of the pool. Every 10 seconds, a swimmer checked the clock and off he went. The workouts were so rigorous that one swimmer would vomit after almost every practice.

During the peak of the frosty Michigan winters, the swimmers would be out of their homes by 5:30 in the morning when it was still dark. Within an hour, they were in the Seaholm pool, chugging through a 2,000-yard workout. Then off to classes before another 4,000 yards in the afternoon. By the time they finished, it was dark once again, prompting the swimmers to refer to themselves as moles because they never saw sunlight. Van Fleet, a pencil jammed above his left ear and the ever-present stopwatch in one hand, would stalk the pool's deck during workouts. "If you don't want to be a state champion or an all-American, I don't want to see you," Van Fleet told his swimmers at the beginning of one season. (25) His wife jokingly told him that ultimately the swimmers would go "as fast as you told them to."

He imposed stern rules, once tossing a swimmer off the team for mooning cars from the back of the team bus. During the swimming season, he prohibited ice skating, snow skiing or dancing, the latter a particularly tough restriction when Seaholm's students loved to dance in their school cafeteria to the Beatles or Beach Boys. When three of his swimmers snuck into an evening dance at the school, they discovered to their consternation that Van Fleet was there as well. Their punishment? Sit out the next three meets. (26)

Yet swimmers flocked to his program, knowing that success at Seaholm opened a path to the best college programs. "I promise you,

19

if you work hard and follow directions, I can get you a four-year college scholarship," Van Fleet told his swimmers. (27) In this chic suburb 15 miles north of Detroit, everybody seemed to belong to a private club or an advanced junior high program, which gave them a chance to swim every day and provided Van Fleet with a ready supply of fresh swimmers. Interest in the sport was so intense that when Seaholm swam against nearby Royal Oak Kimball, school officials at Kimball realized their bleachers could not accommodate more than 1,000 people. So they improvised and made history. They dispatched 1,500 people to a nearby gymnasium, set up a large 9-by-12 screen and broadcast the meet on closed circuit, black-and-white television–the first televised swimming meet ever in Michigan. Kimball students added commentary on their educational radio station and ran a commercial for U.S. savings bonds. "There doesn't seem to be any limit to this thing," said an awed Royal Oak school official. Roddy anchored Seaholm's winning 200-yard freestyle relay as Seaholm handily won, 60-45, for its 39th consecutive victory. (28)

The Henderson kids all had the same tall, slim build, a look inherited from their father Ed. As a young man in 1938, Ed was photographed with his future bride, Helen, and they had the look of a glamorous Hollywood couple; 22-year-old Ed dashing in his white tie and black tails, and 21-year-old Helen equally stunning in an elegant evening dress. Ed's hair was such a dark brown that some assumed it was black. By 1965, his hair was still brown, although his hairline had dramatically receded in the center of his forehead.

As kids, Ed and Helen were academically gifted. Both enrolled at prestigious Duke University in North Carolina. Ed hoped to be a doctor, but dropped out after two years because his family could no longer afford the tuition. Later, everyone just assumed Ed had a college degree, with his voracious appetite for reading, his love of Mozart and Beethoven and his knack for business. Ed always had his eye on something pioneering. When he enlisted in the Navy two weeks after the Japanese attack on Pearl Harbor, he gravitated toward communications and radar, the latter a relatively new development that gave the Americans a major advantage against the

Japanese Navy, which lacked sophisticated radar. He served as a radio technician aboard the minesweeper *Palmer*, a converted four-stack destroyer from World War I. By 1945, he had been promoted to ensign and was radar officer on the brand-new Pierce, an advanced 2,200-ton destroyer.

In 1942, the *Palmer* took part in the Allied invasion of North Africa, which was still controlled by the Nazi-sympathizing Vichy government in France. In a letter to his mother, Ed sounded more like a reporter than a participant. He coolly described details of the invasion, the "brilliant crimson flashes" of American naval fire at night "followed by flaming projectiles cutting an arc across the sky," and culminating in a "terrific flash as the shells hit their objectives." When he joined the *Pierce* more than two years later, the Pacific War against Japan was in its final days. After the Japanese surrender in September 1945, the *Pierce* was ordered to Wakayama off the Inland Sea. When he and the other U.S. sailors were allowed on the Japanese shore, Ed was taken aback at how destitute the Japanese were. Young kids saying "Hello" in English begged for cigarettes. There were few cars, except for a handful of pre-war Buicks and Chevrolets, and oxen carried goods through the middle of muddy streets. Two weeks later, Ed and other *Pierce* crew members landed in Hiroshima, just two months after the atomic bomb obliterated much of the city and killed more than 100,000 people. A shaken Ed looked about the devastated ruins of the city, describing himself in a letter to Helen as a "physical wreck. There's so much to say about yesterday, but I am not prepared to begin a lengthy report at this time," Ed typed. "I believe I will hit my sack and mull this thing over tonight."

A few months later, Ed received orders to return to the United States. He and Helen made their way back to the Detroit area, where they bought a small house on Stanley Boulevard in Birmingham. Still hoping to find money for medical school, Ed worked for the publishing company that Helen's late father launched in 1926. At a time when most Americans kept their food in iceboxes, Helen's father noted the development of electric refrigerators and concluded they were the appliances of the future. He unveiled a trade newspaper devoted solely to giving consumers the latest information on refrigerators. Helen's father kept the newspaper alive through the Great Depression and despite embezzlement by one of his partners. A decade after his death in 1940, the paper still needed a competent hand to direct it. Ed took on that role.

With his passion for novel ideas and his ability as a meticulous reporter, Ed expanded the newspaper into heating and air conditioning. He spun off a separate division to publish books, and in the late 1950s, created a magazine devoted solely to new ways to control air pollution. In that one, Ed was far ahead of contemporary thinking, so far ahead that he could not find enough customers to buy the magazine. But he was still making good money at the company, called Business News, more than enough to move to a larger home on Glenhurst in Birmingham. In 1962, the Hendersons moved one street over to Westwood where they built a brick colonial. Ed learned to pilot his own Cessna II airplane, flying to such faraway places as California and Colorado, visiting Jim at Culver and even allowing Nancy to take the controls in mid-air. (29)

Ed Henderson rarely lost his composure, particularly in front of his kids who couldn't remember ever seeing him cry. He encouraged rather than admonished. When the kids balked at eating vegetables, Ed would say, "Boy this is good. Are you sure don't want to try this?" When he played his beloved Mozart albums, he would exclaim, "Isn't this the most incredible thing you ever heard?"

Because their parents discouraged them from spending more than an hour every day watching television, Roddy, Jim, and Nancy always rooted about for a new sport. They took a liking to riding horses, with Ed Henderson taking them to a ranch in nearby West Bloomfield where they shunned saddles and rode bareback. He loved to tell Nancy that every time she climbed on a horse, he could see the sparkle in her eyes. As a special treat, Ed took them horseback riding in the Garden of the Gods in Colorado Springs. Most summers, as soon as school ended for the kids in June, Ed and Helen drove the family north to Hidden Valley in Michigan's Lower Peninsula. A typical day began with breakfast at 7 followed by water skiing, swimming, horseback riding and golf. The evening would be capped off by dinner in the roomy lodge or a drive into nearby Gaylord for a movie. (30)

They spent the rest of the summer at the Oakland Hills Country Club in Bloomfield Hills, not far from the Hendersons' Birmingham home. The club was home to the famously demanding South course remodeled by Robert Trent Jones. When Ben Hogan won the 1951 U.S. Open at Oakland Hills, he boasted that he finally "brought this monster to its knees" thus giving the course its legendary nickname "Monster." The club was among the first in Michigan to offer an outdoor swimming pool and a full-time summer program, and by Memorial Day kids were splashing about the pool.

Every morning at 10, Roddy and Nancy would head to the pool and swim two hours of laps followed by a shorter workout in the afternoon. Nancy was a gifted freestyler, swimming the 50-yard freestyle in 35.2 seconds, an excellent time for a 13-year-old girl. Between workouts, the kids would splash about, playing water tag or water polo or leaping off the two diving boards. They spent so much time outdoors that they were always sunburned. If they weren't in the pool, they were in the club's basement in a room they nicknamed the "hole," a hideaway from the adults where they could play "Spit" or poker for nickels, dimes and quarters. One of the highlights every summer was the Fourth of July fireworks show. Roddy, Nancy and their friends would plop down in the grass between the 18th green and the swimming pool and watch in wonder as the rockets screeched high into the black sky and exploded in dazzling white, red and blue. The fireworks illuminated everything, allowing Roddy and Nancy to see scores of people watching from outside the club on Maple Road. (31)

For competition, they swam against boys and girls from other clubs, such as the Grosse Pointe Yacht Club or the Detroit Boat Club. In July of 1964, Roddy's Oakland Hills team competed in five separate meets, followed by the club championships in August. Roddy regularly won the blue ribbons, and Helen, as always, carefully saved them. He piled up so many that he easily won the club's best-

23

swimmer trophy. But at the sports banquet in 1964, he handed it to a 13-year-old freestyler, Kevin Trimmer, explaining, "I know how much Kev worked for and wanted this, and I feel he deserves it more than I." (32) It was a generous gesture and another sign that Roddy did not take the sport seriously. The season ended on Labor Day. One summer, the kids were so unwilling to leave they played water tag even as club technicians were draining the pool. (33)

Nancy, the youngest, was dubbed Miss Moho by her mother– "Mind of her Own." She was quieter than Roddy, but had the same enthusiasm for poetry, a talent they appeared to have picked up from their grandmother. As an adult, Nancy developed more sophisticated free verse, but at 13 she assumed all poetry should rhyme. Because she loved to write lyrics or scribble in her diary, she spent hours in her bedroom. She liked to decorate and was constantly rearranging the furniture. She painted the room light green and draped a yellow flowered spread over a double bed made of traditional maple. She had a matching bedside table, desk and dresser, but usually wrote her poetry while sitting on the floor with her back propped against the bed.

On a bulletin board on one wall, she pinned large photographs of the Beatles and Marianne Faithfull, the British rock star whose appearance and singing style appealed to Nancy. She would sit on a golden ottoman and play her acoustic guitar or read the lyrics on album covers. Like Faithful, Nancy had bangs, and her brown hair fell to her waist, earning the predictable nicknames Rapunzel and Lady Godiva. When she leapt off the high diving board at Oakland Hills, her long hair would fly above her head, a sight that delighted her friends.

Nancy treasured Roddy, his seemingly inexhaustible energy and his contrary manner. He would burst into the house with a shout of "Where's Nancy?" and tried to teach his parakeet Quito how to say "Nancy wants a kiss." She especially liked the cute guys Roddy always brought home, particularly Dave Nelson. Even though Nelson was four years older than Nancy, he enjoyed flirting with her, encouraging her to take up bun boarding and urging her to play songs for him on her guitar. At times, Nancy and Roddy had their spats. Once when Ed and Helen were out for the night, Roddy snuck Peachie Barnum over for a couple of hours of kissing in the basement. Ed and Helen had a firm rule: No kids at the house when they were out. When her parents returned, Nancy told them Peachie had been there.

Their friendship was a sharp contrast to the cool relationship their older brother Jim seemed to have with both of them. Though Jim was just three years older than Roddy, the brothers were worlds apart. Jim was disciplined, sober and conscientious. There was the usual jealousy between brothers, as Jim seemed to resent the time Helen had to devote to Roddy because of the mischief he created. But Jim had his own interests—from summers at Culver, to winters swimming at Seaholm, to fraternity life at Michigan State University. Although he knew Roddy was developing into a champion swimmer a faster swimmer, frankly than Jim—he rarely attended any of Roddy's meets at Seaholm.

When the Hendersons made a trip to Hidden Valley in 1964, Jim drove one of the family's two cars and Roddy joined him. The brothers chatted away about school, sports and girls. Jim was surprised, both at himself and with Roddy. The tall and athletic Roddy seemed more mature than the annoying little kid who always seemed to cause trouble. At the end of the four-hour drive, Jim was thinking of Roddy as an equal. He seemed, Jim thought, more of friend. (34)

The Hendersons finished 1964 at a typical frenetic pace. Every day at least one of them seemed to have something to do: The Beatles in concert in downtown Detroit for Nancy; a football Saturday at Michigan State, and of course, Seaholm meets to watch Roddy swim.

On Christmas Eve, Nancy delivered presents to her friends, baked brownies for her dad and then joined Roddy, Jim, Helen and Ed for a sumptuous dinner. The next morning at 8, they were digging through a mountain of presents under the Christmas tree. Nancy got a new ski sweater, electric tooth brush, a purse and a book about John Lennon. That night, Roddy's closest friends, Mike Adair, Bruce

Berridge and Mark Morden, stopped by. Helen lined up Roddy and his three friends in front of the living room fireplace and snapped photos, Roddy wearing a gray v-neck wool sweater, white button-down shirt and a trendy thin tie. Roddy joined his buddies at the Birmingham theater to see the new Peter Sellers film, "The World of Henry Orient." Then back north to Gaylord and the Otsego Club, a private ski resort in the Sturgeon River Valley, where Roddy, naturally, was already a premier skier. They stayed with family friends at a roomy cottage, which had originally been an old one-room schoolhouse, but their plans to stay until New Year's ended when Ed pulled a tendon in his leg. So it was back to Birmingham. (35)

On New Year's Eve, Nancy was coming down with a cold and decided to stay home. She plopped down on her bed and opened her diary. "Well, that's the end of an exciting year of a 13-year-old girl. I must say it has been exciting. About the best year of my life. Good night.'

TWO

"The aviator's daughter"

Roddy was weak from the flu, but there was no question he would swim that day against Central. "You don't leave your big man out of a key meet if he can get you any points at all," Van Fleet told a reporter.(1) Van Fleet's real problem was a virus had swept through the Seaholm swimmers, including Roddy's buddy, Dave Nelson, whose head ached so badly he wondered why he even showed up. Then, as the swimmers went through their warm-ups, Chuck Geggie arrived with worse news: "My dad says I can't swim today." His parents were unhappy with his physics' grade, and he made matters worse when he did not haul out the garbage that week. The Seaholm swimmers were beside themselves. How could Geggie's parents keep him out of such a critical meet?(2) But Van Fleet always warned his swimmers that when "your parents ask you to do something, you've got to do it." Geggie would have won the 200 and 400-yard freestyle events, enough to give Seaholm the victory. Van Fleet sat on the pool deck and re-worked his lineup. He penciled Roddy in the 100 butterfly and 50 freestyle, switched Tom Lawton to the 400 freestyle, a race he rarely swam, and moved Nelson from the backstroke to the 100 freestyle. By the time Van Fleet finished scribbling, he reluctantly concluded that "there wasn't any way" Seaholm could win.(3)

By contrast, Central's swimmers were healthy and rested. Central Coach Paul Vogel had designed his season around beating Seaholm. That week, he reduced his team's workouts, giving them a chance to rest and record their fastest times. Van Fleet had more on his mind than one January meet. He wanted to win the state championship in March. So he stuck to his usual regimen of intense workouts. He wanted his swimmers to record their best times when it mattered–at the state meet.

Peachie Barnum and Sandy Christman were among the thousand people who made their way to the bleachers. They sat across from a floor-to-ceiling wall of glass, which allowed them to see the last hour of daylight. On warm days, the glass sliding doors would open up to a patio and allow the morning sun to illuminate the pool, but this afternoon with the temperature hovering at 11 degrees, the doors were firmly closed. Roddy's mother, who never missed a meet, picked out a seat. At the last moment, Alex Grether, a Seaholm sophomore, plopped down on the bleachers. He had just finished a driver's training course at Seaholm, which included a gory film about auto accidents. He had heard so much about Roddy Henderson. Now he would have a chance to see him swim for the first time.

It had been a day of mounting frustration for Peachie and Sandy. They had three other kids lined up for pizza that evening–Roddy, Mike Adair and Bruce Berridge. But they could not seem to find a sixth. Mike Adair asked Janice Poplack, a sophomore he had a crush on, but she could not make it. That left Peachie and Sandy to work through their own extensive list of friends.

They thought Betsy Brenton, a Seaholm classmate, would be perfect. She had just broken up with her boyfriend. Peachie and Sandy drove to Betsy's house in a newer section of Troy. At first, Betsy agreed to go. But not long after, another girl asked Betsy to see a late movie at the Birmingham Theater. The girl was only a casual friend, but for some inexplicable reason, Betsy said yes. She telephoned Peachie and backed out of the pizza trip.(4)

Undaunted, Peachie called Carol Wollenberg, a close friend. Carol agreed until a guy asked her out on a double date.(5) Peachie and Sandy asked Sandy Clemens, another good friend from their junior high water ballet team. She had a date, too. Peachie next considered Suzanne Witbeck, who lived across the street, even though Suzanne's parents had grounded her. Ever resourceful, Peachie hatched an elaborate scheme: Once Suzanne finished baby-sitting for a neighbor, she would remain at the neighbor's house until Roddy and Peachie picked her up. After eating pizza, they would drive her home. Her parents would never know any better. But as the afternoon wore on,

Suzanne worried that her parents would catch her. The last thing she needed was to get grounded again. So she telephoned Peachie. She couldn't take the chance.(6)

Few of her friends seemed to know how Barbara Jane Barnum got the nickname Peachie, but all agreed it was perfect. You could always tell Peachie was around: Her bubbly laugh, radiant smile and knack of saying something cute or funny. Even in rare moments of anger, she would utter a completely unexpected "Oh rat shit," which would provoke her friends to bouts of giggles. She would tell friends she'd give them the "skinny," which Peachie explained was the "surfing word for latest news." Her favorite expression was "nothing plus nothing equals nothing." One friend called her a "bright piece of sunshine." Her ninth-grade mathematics teacher called her "Peaches and Cream." (7) A fifth-grade teacher liked her so much that she hand wrote a letter saying, "You make me happy to be your teacher each day by your friendly, polite mannerisms, which have also endeared you to the hearts of your classmates."

She had always been Peachie since a few days after her birth. A nurse noticed her golden hair was almost as soft as peach fuzz. Her father Jack loved the nickname, although she tended to refer to herself as Peach. (8)

She was a "teeny little thing," one friend said, so short that she ritually stood in the first row in class photos. She had rich blue eyes, freckles and short blonde hair in a flip with bangs that nearly covered her left eye. On humid days, Peachie's hair frizzed, annoying her to no end because she wanted straight hair. She would wrap her hair around large orange juice cans or ask a friend to iron it. Once, she and her older sister Patty coated their hair with mineral oil. When they awoke the next morning, they discovered to their horror that they couldn't wash it out. They pleaded with their father to let them hide at home, but ever strict, Jack insisted they go to school. (9)

Although Peachie looked more like a cheerleader than an athlete, she opted for sports. She was not as athletic as Sandy Christman–who was known as a "real jock"–but good enough to compete with the Derby water ballet team, one of the few organized school sports at the time for girls. She and Sandy spent their summers on the swimming team at the Birmingham Country Club, where their parents were members. Peachie enjoyed diving, but she also swam and played tennis. She covered herself with baby oil to sunbathe by the pool. When clouds concealed the sun, she poured on in-door tanning cream. She once tried a sun lamp, but all she managed was a bad burn and a visit to her doctor. If not at the club, Peachie and a handful of friends spent lazy afternoons sunning themselves a few miles north of Birmingham on the broad sandy beach at Elizabeth Lake.

She was one of four daughters. Jacquey, the oldest and a 21-year-old junior at Michigan State, was earnest, hard working and graduated near the top of her class at Seaholm. Patty, who had just turned 19 that week, was a freshman at Michigan State and a reckless tomboy, once falling into a truck filled with cement, forcing her exasperated mother to pluck dry cement from her hair. Patty loved attending football games at Michigan State, and when the Spartans earned a trip to the Rose Bowl, Jack sent her a congratulatory telegram and a dozen red roses. Ten-year-old Krisa was the youngest and most athletic, already developing a passion for riding horses. Krisa always seemed to devise new ways to cause trouble. She threw dirtballs at cars from behind the hedge in the Barnum front yard. She used different colored crayons to draw on a family room wall hidden by a large organ, which her horrified parents only discovered on the day they were moving from Kentucky to Michigan. Their mother gave them all two names, figuring if they didn't like one, they could go by the other. So it went: Jacqueline Sue, Patricia Ann, Barbara Jane and Krisa Lynn.

The Barnums lived in a whitewashed center-hall colonial perched on an expansive and slightly raised lot at the corner of Cranbrook and Yarmouth. The house had a circular driveway and a large yard with scores of rose bushes, a dazzling rainbow of yellow, red and pink. The front door led to an entry hall and a staircase, with a small library off to the right and the living room to the left. A breakfast room opened up to the dining room in the rear of the house. The staircase led to a second-floor hallway and small sewing room, where a door provided access to a second-floor balcony with its panoramic view of the courtly mansions on Cranbrook Road. There were four bedrooms upstairs. Their parents had the master bedroom, Jacquey and Patty each kept their own and Peachie and Krisa shared the fourth. When Jacquey and Patty left for Michigan State, Peachie commandeered Jacquey's spacious and coveted corner bedroom facing the backyard.

Somebody was always coming or going at the Barnum house, just "like an open-door policy," Krisa would quip. Fortunately, Betty was well organized and loved to entertain Jack's associates from IBM or any number of kids hanging out with her daughters. She enjoyed cooking, lasagna was one of her favorites. The house was stocked with potato chips, homemade brownies, and Betty's own cheesecake—an improvised recipe that included Lorna Doone cookies, one-half stick of butter, eight ounces of cream cheese, four tablespoons of sugar and one egg.(10)

With four girls, the house seemed to radiate energy. Because Jacquey, Patty and Peachie were separated by less than six years, they often shared clothes, producing the predictable "who's got the white blouse I was going to wear?" The family had a large German shepherd named Hilda and a cat called Penny. Peachie loved Hilda because both were mischievous; Hilda once dashed across the street to a neighbor's house and plucked a large Thanksgiving turkey from the back door where it had been left unguarded to thaw. The girls were expected to care for Hilda, which included cleaning up after her. With her playful sense of humor, Peachie once placed the bag and scooper under Hilda in the hope that the dog would go about her business and save Peachie the chore of picking anything up. (11)

In her cheerfully rebellious manner, Peachie preferred to maneuver around her strict father rather than openly defy him. She would swipe cigarettes from a large drawer. At one of Jack's signature barbecues, Peachie siphoned off some vodka in a glass and almost carried it away before her father sternly asked, "What's in that?" The house rule was no friends over if the parents were out, so

31

naturally, Peachie invited kids over when Jack and Betty were gone. She had great fun until Krisa threatened to tell their parents. What would it cost to keep you quiet, Peachie asked Krisa? A toy horse at a local game shop was the answer. So Peachie bought her an elaborate gray-colored hand-carved wooden horse. Peachie devised a way to defy Jack's rigorous skirt-check: He demanded their skirts brush the kneecap. Within minutes after leaving the house, Peachie would roll up the waist of her skirt up to make it shorter. (12)

The daughters even made up a jingle about themselves and loved to sing out a chorus when friends were around:

"We are the Barnum girls,
We wear our hair in curls,
We wear our dungarees rolled up above our knees,
We're too old for toys, but we're just right for boys."

On her first day at Derby Junior High School in January 1961, Peachie was escorted into a choir class and introduced as Barbara, a 12-year-old whose family had just moved from Kentucky. The music teacher asked a girl near the door to shepherd Peachie around the school. The girl obliged but it quickly became apparent that Peachie needed little help in making friends.(13) In no time, she was in the right clique. "Somebody comes in from out of town and feels out of it," said Tudy Banes, one of Peachie's closest friends. "But she was so easy to be with and so friendly and had this wonderful smile, that she drew people to her."

Peachie's large ensemble of friends constantly gathered together or chatted by telephone. On weekends, they would assemble at one of Birmingham's two movie theaters, usually to see such popular teenage girl films as Sandra Dee in "Tammy Tell Me True." When the Beatles performed in Detroit in 1964, Peachie and her girlfriends cheered themselves hoarse. They made a point of celebrating birthdays, giving each other 45s of the Beatles, Beach Boys or Dion. They hosted Sweet 16 parties for each other, with everyone chipping in to buy an expensive gift such as snow skis. (14)

Peachie also loved hosting sleepovers for her closest girlfriends, always making a point of including Sandy Christman. At one party as a friend clicked away with a camera, Peachie jumped on a chair and burst into a cheery smile. Her mother Betty, who loved to dote on her daughters, arranged rows of sleeping bags in the finished basement, cooked Sloppy Joes and stayed out of their way the rest of the night. The girls munched on popcorn and potato chips, drank pop, gossiped about guys and fiddled with their hairstyles. Her girlfriends asked how she kept her legs so silky smooth, so Peachie demonstrated how she meticulously shaved. They would listen to 45s with racy lyrics, such as "Louie, Louie," which they played over and over until they were sure of the words, "Each night, at 10, I lay her again." If they were lucky, one of the Detroit TV stations would feature a late-night horror film; after watching Vincent Price in "The Fly," one girl was so frightened she complained for weeks of having nightmares. (15) Occasionally, Roddy and a few other boys would telephone, but not for long because this was girls' night out. The girls who fell asleep before dawn were likely to become victims of practical jokes. Sometimes a photo would be taken of them sleeping. Or, friends would heat a bowl of water and place the sleeping girl's hand in it, causing her to awaken with a start and rush to the bathroom. At almost every slumber party, somebody would throw up. In the morning, Peachie's mother prepared a sumptuous breakfast.

To Peachie, school was more an extension of her active social life. Her sisters joked that she majored in having a nice time. At the end of her eighth grade year, she scribbled a note in a friend's yearbook: "Sally: It has really been a riot this year, especially on the bus with our cool bus driver. I can hardly wait 'till camp. I hope we'll have a blast. Good luck always. Love 'ya, Peach." (16)

Peachie was popular enough to quickly gain admission to Derby's exclusive Camp and Trip Club. Only 25 of the Derby girls could join, which gave the club an elitist feel. Every May, the girls would head north for 10 days in the thick woods, usually to the Au Sable River, which wound its way from Grayling across the state until it emptied into Lake Huron. Once they embarked on a three-day, 80-mile canoe trip on the broad river, which included a few hazardous rapids. At night, they pitched tents, built a roaring campfire and roasted "s'mores -- short hand for "I want some more" -- a marshmallow placed on a graham cracker and covered with a Hershey's chocolate square. Then they would sit by the campfire and fix their hair, with Peachie toting along her ever-present orange juice cans in a vain effort to keep her hair straight. She once burst out with "Oh rat shit," prompting the school counselor to admonish her in a good natured manner, "We're not talking like that." (17)

She had a knack for acting and sang in the mixed choir in the eighth and ninth grades. One year at Derby, Peachie and her friends dressed up in sailor uniforms they bought from an Army-Navy surplus store, persuaded one guy to wear a hula skirt and coconut shells over his chest, and sang "Honey Bun" from South Pacific. In April of 1963, she starred in a Gay 90's show at Derby, which included "Can-Can" and "Please Don't Talk to the Lifeguard." Peachie and eight other girls decked themselves out in old-fashioned swimwear – white bloomers, red-and-white striped suits and hat, with no shoes or sandals. Then they gathered on the school gymnasium stage around a muscular member of the boy's swimming team who portrayed the lifeguard.

"Dark and handsome, golden tan,
Six feet tall, man-oh-man!
 Gotta make him mine, all mine
Wish they'd take away that sign
Please don't talk to the lifeguard."

Peachie seemed so absorbed in school plays and so indifferent to schoolwork that her mother feared she would not qualify for college, an absolute requirement for the Barnum daughters. Jack Barnum came from a family that prized education and reading. His grandmother, Nannie Knowlton Barnum was a poet whose book, "Musings," had been published in 1931. His father was a lawyer and his uncle a judge. Jack earned a degree in government and economics from Miami University near Cincinnati and ritually reminded his daughters that college allowed him to become a successful executive at IBM. So Betty Barnum persuaded one of Patty's best friends and a member of the Honor Society at Seaholm, to help as a tutor. The tutor would stop at the Barnum house, where Peachie would be dutifully waiting in the library. Peachie's mother would keep the house quiet while Peachie and her tutor went over algebra, geometry and English. Peachie worked hard during those sessions and it was evident that Peachie eventually would attend Michigan State like her older sisters. (18)

Jack Barnum's friends joked that he lived in a sorority house. He loved all four daughters but seemed to have a special connection with Peachie and Krisa. With their curly blonde hair and blue eyes, Peachie and Krisa resembled their father. At age 48, the trim 5-foot-7 Jack was strikingly handsome–a cross between actor Joseph Cotton and Snooky Lanson, a singer on NBC's "Your Hit Parade."

Jack could be prickly, stern and distant. He was as demanding of his daughters as he was of his employees at IBM. "When he spoke, we ran," Krisa said years later. Before they could go out, they had to make their beds, tend to the roses, polish his Thunderbird or clean up after Hilda. They were taught to display good manners and write thank-you notes when friends did favors. Jack worked long hours and frequently traveled. He could not attend Patty's graduation from Seaholm because he was out of town working. When he was in town, he rarely came home before seven, although Betty always waited for him to arrive home before serving dinner. Jacquey, the oldest and most confident, openly clashed with her father. She pestered Jack to quit smoking cigarettes, prompting him to curtly reply, "If I want to smoke for the rest of my life, I'm going to smoke and you aren't going to convince me otherwise."(19) He was appalled when Jacquey decided to attend Michigan State. The university was too big, he argued. Why wouldn't she go to Miami University in Ohio, a smaller college that he had attended? But Jacquey had her way.

Torry

He had smoother relationships with Peachie and Krisa. They saw past what Krisa later described as "a little bit of a mean streak." Instead, they loved his impish sense of humor and fondness for practical jokes. If Jack liked you, he needled you and seemed to take special delight in sly comments designed to torment or embarrass. He would take Krisa to breakfast and, pretending he owned an airplane, would suddenly announce in a loud voice, "Well, where are we going to fly today?" As people in the restaurant stared, Krisa would squirm uncomfortably and think to herself about hiding under the table. Then Jack would quietly point to different people and maliciously whisper, "Those two over there aren't happily married," or "their kid is adopted."

On weekends, Jack would put work aside and turn to his wide assortment of outdoor grills. A good friend worked for a grill manufacturer and sent Jack the latest models; the girls swore that he had seven at once. With a cigarette in his left hand and a martini in his right, Jack grilled hamburgers and steaks for just about anybody who showed up. He cooked scrumptious potatoes in a cast-iron skillet on the grill and capped off the evening with homemade ice cream, his signature brand being peach. On Sunday mornings, he grilled stacks of pancakes and entertained friends with his snappy sense of humor. Then he spent the day watching pro football on television.

His favorite team was the Cleveland Browns, in part, because his best friend, Gordon Cooper, was a lifelong buddy of the team's storied coach, Paul Brown. Cooper would invite Brown and some of his assistant coaches to his Lake Erie home off Port Clinton. Jack and his family were often there too. Peachie loved the lake, playfully referring to it as Gordon's Lake. When the Browns played the Lions in Detroit, Jack and Gordon hosted Mike McCormick, the sturdy Cleveland offensive tackle, at the Barnum house for a post-game dinner.

The book about their dad rested on a shelf in the first-floor library, the room where Peachie studied so diligently with her tutor.

Written in 1943 by Ira Wolfert, "Torpedo 8" had been a bestseller during World War II. It was the story of the most fabled U.S. air squadron of World War II. Torpedo Squadron 8 was featured on the cover of Life Magazine and later attracted the attention of such prominent writers as Walter Lord and John Toland. Krisa knew her father's name was scattered throughout the book, but he never spoke about it and she hesitated to ask. Jack was a pilot in Torpedo Squadron 8, but because of a simple twist of fate, he and a handful of other pilots were not with the rest of the squadron in June of 1942 when every single plane was shot down during a daring attack on four Japanese aircraft carriers during the battle of Midway. Instead, Jack inherited the task of explaining to the widows and girlfriends at Pearl Harbor that their husbands and boyfriends would not be coming home.

Jack joined the Navy in 1940 at the age of 23, after graduation from Miami University and a short stint at a job in Youngstown. But he was too restless to remain an accountant, particularly as war raged in Europe between the Germans and British. He admired British Prime Minister Winston Churchill and President Franklin D. Roosevelt, predicting long before the U.S. entered the war that "it will be the combined efforts of these two men which will ultimately defeat Hitler."(20) He enlisted in the Navy, underwent basic training at Grosse Ile Naval Station in Detroit, and attended flying school at the Naval Air Station in Pensacola. He loved the warm Florida temperatures, the spanking new barracks with fresh mattresses and pillows, the nightly films shown at the base, such as "The Philadelphia Story," and the new clothes given to him–three pairs of shoes, six shirts and a starched white dress suit with brass buttons. He always seemed to find a new girl. "I've never been so happy in all my life," Jack wrote his father. (21) He trained to fly the Devastator torpedo bomber, designed to skim near the water's surface and launch a torpedo against enemy shipping. In its day, the Devastator was a remarkable technological development, but by 1942 it was hopelessly obsolete, too slow to fend off the swifter Japanese Zeros.

Jack, who was nicknamed Barney by the other pilots, was assigned to Torpedo Squadron 8. They were a hardy group, these young pilots from such faraway places as Louisiana, Ohio and Alabama. They were told their chief objective was to live long enough to fire their torpedoes and their second goal was to get back to the carrier alive. When the aircraft carrier *Hornet* and most of Torpedo Squadron 8 sailed to the Pacific in 1942, Jack and a handful of pilots stayed behind in Norfolk to take delivery of the brand-new Avenger torpedo bomber, a more advanced and faster replacement for the poky Devastator. Jack and his five comrades flew their Avengers to Pearl Harbor only to discover that the *Hornet* had already left to engage a huge Japanese fleet amassing off Midway Island. While at Pearl Harbor, Jack heard the appalling news that all 15 Devastators taking part in the attack had been shot down and only one of the 30 crew members survived. At Pearl Harbor, Jack and the remaining squadron pilots vowed revenge. "Torpedo 8 still exists," Swede Larsen, the squadron's executive officer, told Jack and the other pilots. "We've got a score to settle and a chance to settle it."(22)

By August, the reconstituted Torpedo Squadron 8 was assigned to the aircraft carrier *Saratoga,* which was covering the Marines landing on Guadalcanal. On the evening of August 7, Jack and three other Avengers armed with bombs took off from the *Saratoga* to provide air cover for U.S. Marines on Guadalcanal. Unable to reach the ground commander by radio, Jack radioed the American commander on nearby Tulagi Island and volunteered to help in any way. The Tulagi commander ordered Jack and his planes to attack Japanese positions on a nearby island. The four planes launched a series of attacks, setting afire key oil depots, strafing Japanese troops and earning Jack a letter of commendation.(23)

A couple of weeks later, Jack was flying one of five Avengers, when in the early evening they spotted five Japanese heavy cruisers, one light cruiser, a seaplane carrier and six sleek destroyers, their black superstructures plainly visible against the golden glow of the setting sun. "Get the nearest big one," Larsen shouted through the radio. Jack could see the orange bursts of anti-aircraft fire, which one pilot later described as looking like a swarm of fireflies. Jack's Avenger shuddered from a hit, which disabled his radio. Jack and the other four pilots glided their torpedo bombers toward the safety of a bank of clouds and emerged just northwest of the Japanese ships to drop their torpedoes. Once clear of the Japanese task force, the Avengers headed back to the *Saratoga*. It was dark and Jack marveled at how large the Pacific Ocean was, particularly to a pilot short on fuel, without a radio and uncertain of his exact position.(24) Two of the Avengers ditched in the water where the crews were later rescued, but Jack and the other two planes reached the safety of the *Saratoga*. When he examined the plane, he discovered several holes from anti-aircraft fire, including one that measured a foot in diameter. He was awarded the Navy Cross, with the citation hailing Jack for "pressing home his attack through a bursting hail of fire from hostile anti-aircraft batteries." (25)

When Jack wasn't flying off the *Saratoga,* he was stationed on Guadalcanal at Henderson Field, a makeshift old Japanese landing strip.
Breakfast often consisted of prunes and crackers. Dinner was beans and canned meat, although once Jack was lucky enough to find a bottle of Japanese beer, which he said "didn't taste so bad." Just about every night, Jack ducked into a foxhole to avoid Japanese gunfire or bombs; he spent one long night in a foxhole in the company of a jungle rat. (26)

When he returned to the United States and left the Navy, Jack had lucrative offers to fly commercial aircraft. Instead, he opted to accept a smaller salary to join IBM, the computer giant that would become the nation's sixth largest company. Jack became friends with the legendary IBM president Thomas Watson, Jr., who also had flown in World War II. Jack was smart, ambitious and worked hard. He was a demanding supervisor who challenged younger workers when they proposed new ideas. He wanted his sales representatives to be as addicted to hard work as he was. The long hours and stress came with a price: Jack aggravated the painful ulcers he had suffered from since high school. He earned a series of promotions, although each one required a move to a new city, prompting one daughter to quip that IBM stood for "I'm Being Moved." First Pittsburgh. Then nearby Johnstown. Next Louisville, where the girls loved watching a powerfully built teenager and future boxing star Muhammad Ali clip their lawn. Finally Detroit, where Jack and Betty moved into the fashionable Birmingham section off Cranbrook Road.

Jack and Betty joined the Birmingham Country Club because it was a handy place to have dinner after a long day of work. Betty polished her golf game and joined the club's golf committee. Betty was bright enough that had she been born in the 1950s, she might well have attended college and found a full-time job, prompting her daughters to commiserate that she had been born too early. Instead, she focused on being a homemaker. She was a skilled artist and enjoyed taking part in community plays, a trait she passed on to Peachie. She played the violin. She entertained everyone by playing her favorite 1940s songs on a large organ in the living room. Betty was the one the girls turned to for help because she seemed, in the words of one daughter, the consummate mother. When Krisa rode horses at a stable in Novi, Betty would make the 45-minute drive every day. She arranged for an artist to paint portraits of her daughters. When it was Peachie's turn at age 5, Betty dressed her in a sparkling blue dress and instructed her to adopt a serious pose, one of the rare times in Peachie's life she did not smile. In a special touch, Betty gave each daughter a unique present to wear around the house or take to bed—a blanket or old cashmere sweater that they nicknamed a "gooey." Peachie's was a tattered rust and black blanket that almost became unidentifiable. But she was attached to the blanket, and once on a long trip inadvertently left it in a motel room. She pleaded with the friend driving the car to return to the motel so she could fetch her gooey.

The summer before Jacquey went to Michigan State in 1962, Jack and Betty gathered up the four daughters for the seven-hour drive to the French Lick spa in Indiana. Jacquey and Patty soon would be off to Michigan State and Jack and Betty were not certain they would ever vacation again as a family. The girls loved the turn-of-the-century resort, complete with lush colorful gardens, boat rides, mineral springs and ornamental gazebo. Their futures, like those of most everyone in Birmingham, seemed limitless. There was talk of another big promotion for Jack: Perhaps even a move abroad.

Peachie, Roddy and their friends were the lucky ones. Though their parents had grown up without much money, through hard work, smarts and ingenuity they became successful professionally: Sandy Christman's father Dale was an osteopathic surgeon, Mike Adair's dad an obstetrician, and Bruce Berridge's father helped run a company that sold brake line tubes to the auto companies. Jack Barnum jokingly called his neighborhood the "Cranbrook Yarmouth Cultural Society"–part of a suburb of twisting roads, lush green yards and stately maples and oaks.

They all lived within a few-block radius of each other. Roddy's parents owned a redbrick colonial with a large bay window and two white pillars framing the front door. Bruce lived down the street in a colonial, while Mike Adair's house was several streets over on Puritan. Sandy Christman grew up in a brick colonial on Yarmouth Road where it formed a triangle with Cranbrook. From her front door, Sandy could look directly across the triangle at Peachie's house. If their homes were much alike, so were their lives and expectations. Donna Richardson, one of Peachie's close friends, "just assumed every family had two televisions and two cars." For Christmas in 1964, Jack bought Betty a sheared beaver coat. Peachie grabbed sunglasses, shoved on a pair of black boots and modeled the coat, striking a glamour pose. As a matter of course, it was simply expected that everyone would attend college. Kids grew up convinced that "nothing bad happens to you in Birmingham except a bad report card and your parents are mad at you."(27)

Their hangout was uptown Birmingham, a trendy collection of boutiques, art galleries, restaurants and clothing stores just 15 miles north of Detroit. The epicenter was the intersection of Maple Road and Woodward Avenue. Peachie and her friends would stop by the Villager Store, where girls bought their plaid kilts and matching cardigan wool sweaters and knee socks, or they'd head to Baker's for nylons and shoes. For the boys, it was the Prep Shop on Pierce Street, where they could find the latest button-down shirts or V-neck wool sweaters, matching them with tight white Levi's and penny loafers –without the penny, of course. Farther down the street, you could buy gym uniforms and swim suits at the Varsity Shop, while just next door was Games Imported, the toyshop owned by the father of one of Mike's girlfriends where many of the boys found part-time jobs. There also was a lingerie shop that Roddy called the "boner store," where he checked out the latest bras on the mannequins. After school, kids mingled in large groups at the soda fountain at Kresge's at the corner of Maple and Henrietta. The more audacious girls would sneak into the basement bathroom at Jacobson's department store where they could smoke cigarettes without fear of being caught. Sometimes they stopped at Demery's department store, where the girls dropped off their books, and planned weekend parties.

Some kids spent their evenings at the Raven Gallery, which Nancy Henderson wrote was a "place where everybody goes." The Raven had soft drinks, coffee and folksingers strumming their guitars. But more often than not, the kids ended up at the home of Ellen Tower, who went steady with Bruce and Roddy–every girl seemed to have been out with Roddy at least once. Ellen's father dug a pit in the backyard and covered the hole with a ground-level trampoline. That way, he explained, there was less chance anyone would get hurt. On hot summer nights, Ellen and her girlfriends slept on the trampoline. The girls called themselves the "Fly By Nights," because they would fly about the neighborhood at night in search of friends or basement parties. "We really love 'ya for your tramp," one friend scribbled in Ellen's ninth-grade Barnum yearbook. (28)

In a state of large lakes and steep hills, there was always something to do in summer or winter. On the last day of classes at Seaholm in the spring of 1964, Bill Keough commandeered his mother's Pontiac and drove Roddy, Mike and Bruce north for a canoe trip–"just a bunch of goof-offs" having a memorable day. They roared up Interstate 75 at a high speed, at times screeching past 100 miles per hour. But then nobody would have worried. Kids, they knew, were indestructible. (29)

By the fall of 1963, Peachie seemed busier then ever. She volunteered to work on the sophomore class's entry for Field Day, a storied Seaholm tradition that served as Homecoming. Each class made up its own theme, designed an imposing banner, created individual outfits and wrote catchy tunes. Three-legged races, tug-of-war, egg throws and a sack race capped off the day, with the winning class taking the coveted Cider Barrel. The competition among the seniors, juniors and sophomores was ruthless, for no senior class wanted to suffer the indignity of losing Field Day to the underclass boys and girls.

As the graduation class of 1966, Peachie and her friends planned their Field Day show around Route 66, the TV hit in which actors Martin Milner and George Maharis drove their 1960 Corvette from Chicago to Los Angeles. They designed a banner of the United States complete with a line drawn from the Midwest to California and the words, "Destination Graduation." Each student wore a smaller banner with Route 66 on it. Then they adapted Nelson Riddle's recording of the show's theme music and sang away:

"While driving on Route 66,
We came upon Field Day.
The junior and the senior class,
Both could hear us say.
We've got to beat those upperclassmen.
And show that we're the tops."(30)

Peachie met Roddy that fall and within no time were an item. "She was smitten with him from the time she met him," said one friend.(31) In many ways, they were the perfect couple–the coolest guy going out with the most popular girl. It was like watching Ken and Barbie, thought Donna Richardson. They had it all: Good looks, intelligence and sassy personalities. They were mischievous without being malicious. They loved to tease each other. When Roddy and

Dave Nelson went to downtown Detroit to see the burlesque star Peaches O'Day perform, Roddy quickly attached the name to Peachie. The only mismatch was Roddy towering over tiny Peachie, prompting Jacquey to quip they looked like Mutt and Jeff. She spent much of her free time with Roddy, becoming a regular at every Seaholm meet. At Christmas in 1964, Roddy bought Peachie a necklace, although he fretted to his mother, "I don't know if it's going to fit her very well." (32)

It took Roddy's strong personality to put up with Jack Barnum. Boys interested in his daughters had to run a gauntlet because Jack peppered them with so many questions that the girls grumbled about his third degree. When one of Patty's boyfriends arrived to pick her up for a date, Jack looked at him with clear disapproval and snorted, "That's an ugly tie." If by chance Sandy Christman's father was at the Barnums, he and Jack would grill any guy who had the misfortune to stop by.

Yet Peachie was not certain if Roddy would be a lasting boyfriend. She fretted that he showed interest in another girl. She worried about the memory of Anne Le Fevre. Anne and her family moved to Chicago during Peachie's sophomore year. But Anne still had a crush on Roddy, and Roddy seemed to reciprocate. When Anne visited Birmingham for a few days in the fall of 1964, she went back to Seaholm. Peachie spied her in the school cafeteria.

"Do you still like him?" Peachie asked. Yes, Anne replied. She and Roddy exchanged letters and spoke by telephone.

"I think he likes you, but I really want him to like me," Peachie said.(33)

The doubts she expressed to Anne revealed a side of Peachie few ever saw. She looked with envy at girls who were taller and more slender. She disliked her wavy hair and constantly changed its style. In the eighth grade, she clipped her hair short with tiny bangs. A year later, she grew her hair longer into a bubble style. To only her closest friends she fussed that she was fat and not attractive enough. "It bothered me that she felt that badly," one friend said.(34) While at Derby, Peachie seemed plump, almost pudgy. But by her sophomore year at Seaholm, she shed much of the extra weight. She stood in the front row for her homeroom class photo, her hair flawlessly coifed and her face beaming with a radiant smile. In a class filled with cute girls, she was the prettiest.

During the first few days of 1965, Peachie seemed unusually lonely. With Jacquey and Patty off to winter classes at Michigan State and Sandy Christman scuba diving in Mexico, she complained that the Barnum house seemed dead. She went out with Roddy, although she had qualms about their future. But she perked up with the thought of Sandy returning. On the day before Sandy's arrival, Peachie and a good friend used a spare key to sneak into Sandy's house and decorate her bedroom with "Welcome home" signs. Then the mischievous Peachie wrapped toilet paper around the room to create what she called "a wreck." The next night in a letter to her sister Patty, she scribbled, "Sandy gets home in an hour and I'm really excited." She concluded with, "Well, I suppose I should get back to the books–pretty poor excuse for writing such a short letter, but couldn't think of anything else. Love, Peach."

It was so cold the Friday before the Saturday swimming meet, that Peachie cheerfully accepted an offer from some girlfriends for the short ride from Seaholm to her house. She was excited about the swimming meet. Did any of them want to go, she kept asking? Then as the car pulled up to the Barnum home, its front yard covered with fresh snow that glowed in the early evening, Peachie jumped out. She disappeared through the front door.(35)

THREE

"The Jokester"

The meet began badly for Seaholm. Central won the opening 200-medley relay, setting a Seaholm pool record. Tom Lawton swam the 200 freestyle in 1:55.4 to give Seaholm a victory, but a physically weakened Roddy finished fourth in the 50 freestyle, one of the few times in his life he failed to score a point. Helen Henderson, sitting in the bleachers and armed with her customary scoring sheet, was so disappointed she could not bring herself to scrawl Roddy's time or finish. (1)

The diving competition followed, giving Roddy time to recover his strength for his next event, the 100 butterfly. Van Fleet matched him against Ted Blakeslee, a senior co-captain who had not lost all year. Roddy had yet to swim the butterfly in a competitive high school meet, but Van Fleet assured a skeptical reporter that "Rod could swim any event in the book for us and he might win it." (2) As Blakeslee touched the wall first at the finish, he glanced in astonishment to the next lane where Roddy had finished a close second. A healthy Roddy would have won, Blakeslee thought. (3)

Seaholm placed first and third in the 100 backstroke with Mike Adair posting the best time of his life, nearly breaking one minute. But with one event left–the 200-freestyle relay–Seaholm's lead was shaved to one point. At this moment, high school rules worked against Van Fleet. Roddy had already competed in two events and was not eligible for a third. Deprived of his best sprinter, Van Fleet cobbled together a makeshift relay. The race was close, but Central narrowly won. A frustrated Helen didn't pencil in the winning time or the meet's final score.

The 48-meet winning streak was a thing of the past. The Seaholm swimmers, who had thought they were invincible, were stunned– "bummed out," Chuck Geggie later said. But Van Fleet was not discouraged. He knew Seaholm would qualify more swimmers than

Central for the state meet. And he would have Roddy, Michigan's premier swimmer.

Never one to dwell on a loss, Roddy showered, dressed and put the meet behind him. He wanted to join Peachie and his friends. Knowing that Peachie had yet to find a sixth kid, Roddy impulsively asked Dave Nelson to go along. Nelson shuddered. He was so sick from the flu that all he wanted to do was go home and climb into bed. That left Roddy, Peachie, Sandy, Bruce and Mike. Roddy drove them the short distance from the Seaholm parking lot to Sandy's house, where the three boys stayed long enough to chat with Sandy's father, who was privately delighted. His oldest daughter was starting to show a real interest in guys. Roddy, Bruce and Mike seemed just right. Then the boys left. In a couple of hours, they planned to return and collect Peachie and Sandy to go out for pizza. (4)

By the time Mike Adair got home from the meet, he was ravenous. He ate spaghetti with his family and then pulled on corduroy Levi's, black boots, a Michigan State University football jersey with a green numeral 69–a trendy sexual joke–and his maroon Seaholm varsity letter jacket. Like Roddy, Mike had forgotten about the loss and was happy to get out of the house. In particular, he was looking forward to getting to know Peachie. When they passed each other in the school halls, Mike had been too bashful to say hello. "This is going to be great," Mike told himself. He knew Peachie would become a close friend.

He borrowed his mother's Buick station wagon, dropped off his younger sister Nancy at a friend's house and drove across Maple to the triangle formed by Yarmouth and Cranbrook. The soft white lights of the Christman and Barnum homes twinkled in the early evening, adding a glow to the snow-covered lawns.

Roddy was there already. It had been a particularly lucky night for him because he had his mother's burgundy Skylark. His older brother Jim wanted the car for a fraternity rush party at Michigan State, explaining to his dad that there was always a shortage of cars during rush week. But the last thing Ed wanted was a bunch of drunken college students driving the family car.(5)

Roddy and Peachie jumped into the front seat, while Bruce, Mike and Sandy slid into the back. Roddy could have driven east on Yarmouth and linked up with Oak Street, a broad sidestreet that ran parallel to Maple and usually was free of traffic. When Roddy's friend Mark Morden drove his buddies uptown, he invariably took Oak. But Roddy selected the most direct route to Birmingham, turning the Skylark south on Cranbrook until he reached Maple. There he took a left, heading uptown. At the intersection of Maple and Woodward, Roddy turned right. The pizza parlor was just a mile and one-half away.(6)

Roddy hadn't been driving very long. He got his prized driver's license four months earlier on his 16th birthday – September 29, 1964, an event of such importance that Nancy Henderson entered it in her diary. Within a couple of weeks, Roddy was driving his father and Nancy up Woodward to Ted's, a favorite drive-in gathering place for kids.(7) Roddy conscientiously obeyed speed limits. But rather than scrupulously watching the road, he tended to chatter with those in the car. He loved to search the radio for "Dance, Dance, Dance," released that October by the Beach Boys:

Getting a license freed kids from the grips of their parents and allowed them to go "Woodwarding," racing up and down the broad avenue that linked downtown Detroit to the northern suburbs of Birmingham and Bloomfield Hills. Woodward had eight lanes–four southbound to Detroit and four northbound to Bloomfield Hills. A wide median of grass and trees separated the southbound and northbound lanes, creating an avenue so wide that it was difficult to make left-hand turns. So state officials compensated with a complicated maneuver that became known as the "Michigan Left." To make a left off Big Beaver Road onto Woodward, you had to first turn right and head north on Woodward, then quickly steer into the left lane until you reached a turnaround in the median. There, it was left into the southbound lanes.

By 1965, Woodwarding was the rage for high school kids. They cruised Woodward in search of guys and girls, driving as far north as Ted's on Square Lake Road and as far south as 10 Mile Road to the

49

Totem Pole, a drive-in known for its Big Chief cheeseburger. For the boys, the trick was to get a glib, good-looking guy in the shotgun seat, where he could attract girls in other cars and think of something clever to say. At 50 miles per hour, these conversations went on and on until the guys could persuade the girls to stop for hamburgers, cokes or milk shakes. Teenage use of grass and acid was a couple of years away, but a number of Seaholm kids drank beer and smoked cigarettes. There were make-out parties, and teenagers kissed and petted, but it was still two years before the summer of love at Haight-Ashbury. High school students were becoming more interested in national politics, but the conflict in Vietnam still seemed far away. The U.S. buildup in Vietnam would not reach 184,000 troops until the end of 1965, and as the year began few kids were protesting the war.

Woodward was one of the main throughways to Detroit. In the days before the 1967 riots, Detroit was the nation's fifth largest city, eclipsed in population only by New York, Los Angeles, Chicago and Philadelphia. More than 1.6 million of the metro area's 4.2 million people lived within Detroit's city limits. You could still ride the train from Birmingham to downtown Detroit, but by 1965, most people either took Woodward to the central part of the city, or Southfield Road, which connected uptown Birmingham to Dearborn and Detroit. The car and Detroit were inextricably linked. Just about everybody had a connection to the auto industry. In April of 1964, Ford introduced the Mustang, the sleek sports car with the flair of the Ferrari and a $2,368 price tag that made it accessible to everyone. The car was such a hit that Ford sold 400,000 during the first year, boosting the company's annual sales by 10 percent and increasing its market share to nearly 28 percent.

The heart of Detroit was a magnet, with its wide selection of shops, restaurants and theaters. Canadians from Toronto found Detroit nightlife a lively contrast to their tidy, but dull city, and they flocked there for weekends. The Metropolitan Opera was often a sellout, and people assembled at the Fisher Theatre to see the latest plays. Hudson's, the city's landmark department store, attracted shoppers from downtown as well as the suburbs.

If Roddy was Mr. Cool, Mike Adair was the jokester. One friend dubbed him the class mascot. "You're a riot to be with," another told him. Yet another described him as "a panic." (8) He was a magnet for nicknames, such as Mouse, because he was the shortest guy in every class, or Brillo because of his curly, dark brown hair. The caddy master at the Birmingham Country Club called him Hair. Everybody liked to tease him because they knew he could take it. One girl who went steady with Mike in the eighth grade wrote a note in his yearbook declaring, "You're one of the nicest boys I know. No–I'm just kidding. You're one of the cutest guys I know. No – I'm really kidding there. You are the most popular boy I know (boy, I must be going crazy). But there's one thing I can say for you–just one thing, though. And that's you have big, brown, lovable eyes." Another girl scribbled a yearbook note: "To a cool, nice, terrific, suave, cute, sweet, tall, marvelous guy. The only reason for saying all those things is because you told me to." Only rarely would he show anger at a slight. Once as he danced with a taller girl, she mentioned that his head was resting on her shoulder. "I'm not going to dance with you anymore," Mike snapped and walked away.

On a frigid New Year's Day with nothing better to do, Mike persuaded Bruce Berridge, Mark Morden and Nancy Ackerly to play golf at Orchard Lake Country Club. Nancy watched those "goofballs" whacking golf balls about the frozen fairways. During a party at one girl's house on a winter night, Mike took off his shoes and socks and ran outside in the snow. (9) When they were in the ninth grade, Mike, Roddy, Bruce and the rest of the swimmers performed a gag routine during intermission at the spring water ballet performance. They fastened girls' bathing caps on their hands, wore two-piece bathing suits, and, with Mike leading the way, ran out to the pool to the laughter and applause of the crowd. Then they held hands and one after another dove into the pool, just as if they were performing a water ballet routine.

Torry

One hot summer night as Mike and his buddies slept outside next to a pool in a friend's backyard, they began daring one another to strip and dash down the street. Off the boys went, one by one, running the one-half mile down Pleasant Street to Maple. Because it was three in the morning, there was little chance of getting caught, but Mike hid in the bushes when an occasional car rolled by. They dubbed themselves the BBNC, which stood for the Birmingham Boys Nature Club. Every guy who took part signed his name to a beat-up and nearly deflated basketball. The BBNC became folklore at Barnum, although not everyone seemed to know exactly what the club was about. When one girl wondered how she could join, Bruce slyly asked Mike, "You don't think anyone will mind, do you?" (10)

His full name was Robin Michael Adair, although everyone called him Mike. He looked and acted like his father Robin, a man who used words with economy. Mike was quiet, particularly when first meeting people, almost as if he were preoccupied studying everyone. But once past the initial introductions, he showed a dry sense of humor and was always in search of a laugh. "When you're riding a pony, you'll think of Tony," he scribbled in one girl's 7th grade yearbook, a reference to her boyfriend. (11) At times, it was difficult to tell if he was kidding. When asked why he preferred backstroke, he explained it was the only stroke where he could keep his face dry and breathe easily, saying with a straight face, "Breathing is important." Because he could not see the pool wall while swimming on his back, he occasionally slammed his head into the wall, which he jokingly told friends "explains a lot of things" about him.

He was adept at thinking of clever nicknames for his friends and family. He tagged Susie Martin with the nickname "Legs" which guys thought were the best-looking at Seaholm. When Sally Splane drove her car over a chipmunk, friends started calling her "Killer," a particularly cruel moniker for someone who loved animals as much as she did. When somebody painted Killer on a nearby bridge, Sally was certain, absolutely certain, that Mike was behind the gag. (12)

Mike didn't have Roddy's magnetic charm or Bruce's all-American looks. But girls thought Mike was boyishly cute, almost as if he were a couple years younger than his buddies. The family joke was that every year Mike had a new girlfriend. As a junior, Mike dated Janice Poplack, a Seaholm sophomore he had known since elementary school. Janice was bright and energetic, managing the campaign of a junior running for class office. But like Mike, she was reserved, and uncertain that Mike liked her as much as she liked him. When Mike worked up the courage to ask her out, they double-dated to a drive-in movie. As the other couple made out in the back seat, Mike slipped his arm on to Janice's shoulder, but to her relief, no farther. She decided he was a real gentleman. (13)

If not out with a girl, Mike could be found with Bruce, Roddy and Mark Morden. During one summer morning in 1962, Mike, Bruce and Mark showed up unannounced at one girl's house and persuaded her to make breakfast. She later joked that "you poor guys had to eat it, too." (14)

Although Mike had known Bruce since elementary school, they did not become best of buddies until the eighth grade at Barnum. They joined the glee club and swam on the boy's team. When they took French class, they referred to each other as Michel and Pierre. They were inseparable: From partying at Ellen Tower's house to playing rock singer Jack Scott's records at a friend's house to double-dating. They even found part-time jobs together. They worked for Susie Martin's father in his game store on Pierce Street. To get hired, it helped to have dated Susie, as both Mike and Bruce had. They worked weekends and holidays stocking the shelves with his imported games and toys, such as wood jigsaw puzzles, rocking horses, lead soldiers and stuffed bears. The hours were grueling, prompting Susie years later to tease that her father deliberately designed long workdays so the boys would be too exhausted to make out later with her.(15)

Mike always seemed accident-prone. As a second grader, Mike and other friends lined up to ride a pony at a fair held at a nearby elementary school. The pony broke loose and knocked Mike unconscious. When he awoke, his nose was covered with blood. A teacher stopped the bleeding, but doctors at the hospital missed the fact that he broke his nose. It healed crooked, prompting Bruce Berridge to refer to it as his funny-looking nose. (16)

He was the only one of six Adair kids who ever broke a bone. For years he bounced between fractures and stitches. In the third grade, he broke his left arm while jumping over a rope in his living room. In the eighth grade, he fractured his right arm while, of all things, watching a soccer game. Someone kicked the ball in his direction, and Mike, ever thoughtful, scooped it up to kick it back. One of the players mistakenly assumed Mike was in the game and slammed Mike backwards. He once crashed through a glass door at Bruce Berridge's house and sliced his right wrist and punctured his palm. During his last year at junior high, a doctor surgically removed a wart from his wrist and stitched it up. When the doctor took off the stitches, Mike promptly split it back open while whacking a volleyball in gym class. A year later as a sophomore at Seaholm, he broke a bone in his foot.

Mike spoke of going to medical school, in part because his father was a physician. He earned solid, if not spectacular grades, particularly in the sciences he needed to be a physician. He cracked that his favorite course was gym because he aced it, but in fact he was a good student, often helping friends with algebra in the ninth grade. He learned faster by doing rather than reading, much like his grandfather who at the turn of the century carved elaborate wooden patterns into the Ford cars manufactured in Detroit. Mike once took a file to a piece of mahogany and created a flashy bun board. When his father Robin saw the board, he said, "My dad liked to do stuff like that." (17)

Like just about every kid in Birmingham, Mike was addicted to sports. During junior high school, he caddied at the Birmingham Country Club, a short bike ride from his house. He consistently shot in the low 90s, and except for once throwing a club at Orchard Lake Country Club, he rarely erupted in anger after a bad shot. He simply moved on to the next one. "He absolutely loved the game," one close friend remembered. (18) When Oakland Hills hosted the U.S. Open in 1961, Mike snagged several autographs, including Arnold Palmer's and Don January's. When he asked Ben Hogan to sign his program, though, the legendary golfer put his arm on Mike's shoulder and politely replied, "Sorry son, I don't give autographs."

Mike learned to swim after his family joined Orchard Lake Country Club, perched on the edge of one of the scores of fresh water lakes scattered through suburban Detroit. From the moment school ended in June, Mike and two of his sisters spent much of their summer at the club. The girls learned to play tennis while Mike absorbed golf lessons. Orchard Lake had yet to construct a pool, but club officials built a long dock, sliding board, pair of diving boards and swimming lanes, allowing Mike and his sisters to splash about in the lake's chilly water. The goal was to earn a "fish," an emblem sewn to your suit. If you had a fish, you could swim in the deeper water.

When everyone else swam freestyle at a summer camp event in Michigan's Upper Peninsula, Mike opted for backstroke. Why in the world are you doing that, someone finally asked? "Because I can swim faster that way," Mike explained.

Mike joined Barnum Junior High's swimming team, which included Roddy, Bruce and Bill Crandell. Mike and Crandell competed against each other for the honor of being the team's second best backstroker, although, as always, Mike couldn't help but drive his coach loopy. At the time, only two swimmers from each team competed for points in a meet, but a third could swim for exhibition. The Barnum coach chose Mike for exhibition and Crandell for points, and invariably Mike would win. Deciding to outwit the two, the coach switched them, putting Crandell in exhibition. This time, Crandell finished ahead of Mike.

Mike won all his events as a Barnum ninth grader and served as team co-captain with Roddy. His swimming coach at Barnum predicted he would break one minute in the 100 backstroke by the time he got to Seaholm.(19) At the Ann Arbor Pioneer relays as a Seaholm sophomore, Mike posted the fastest time of any sophomore in Michigan in the 100 backstroke and by his junior year, he was the second-fastest backstroker on the team and appeared certain to finish in the top six at the state meet. One friend quipped that if Mike wasn't the fastest backstroker in Michigan, he at least was the fastest on his street. (20)

Yet Mike shared Roddy's indifference about competitive swimming. They both maneuvered around Van Fleet's rules, particularly the coach's insistence they drink his terrible milk shakes. Instead, Roddy, Mike and Dave Nelson would sneak over to a beef buffet uptown and chow down on roast beef, mashed potatoes and squares of Jell-O. Mike regularly joined Roddy in playing jacks on the deck. The hours spent swimming were too long, and he disliked his wet hair freezing in the icy wind after practice. Although Van Fleet thought Mike was good enough to earn at least a partial athletic scholarship at a small college, Mike only toyed with the idea of collegiate swimming. He planned to enroll at Albion College, a liberal arts college in southern Michigan that his parents attended, and take the demanding courses needed for medical school. He was going to be a doctor. Just like his dad.

Mike's parents were an attraction of opposites. His father Robin was quiet. Mike's mother Betty thought that was "why the ladies liked him because he'd listen to them." Betty was one who needed listening to: She was a self-described "yackety-yak," with a take-charge personality and a sly wit, who at 89 liked to say, "I'm doing pretty well for an old babe." Robin was a passionate golfer who taught himself the game by studying the best golfers he caddied for as a kid. When Betty took up golf, Robin ushered her to a nine-hole course. Betty grew so disgusted at her inability to hit the ball that she threw a golf club and stormed off the course, an absolute violation of Robin's sense of golf etiquette. "That's no way to act on a golf course," Robin chastised her. "You can be frustrated and all that stuff, but you don't show it by doing something as stupid as that." Betty stuck to the game, never tossed a club again and became so skilled that she won a medal at the family country club.(21)

They met in the 1930s as undergraduates at Albion College. After they married, Robin attended medical school at Wayne State University in Detroit while working nights at a factory. Betty found a job teaching at Royal Oak, and by her third year she earned $1,350 annually. When Robin finished his residency in 1943, he joined the Army, did basic training and was assigned to Australia as a military surgeon. For two years, he served in New Guinea followed by a six-month stint in the Philippines. In January of 1946, Major Adair returned to the United States, re-uniting with Betty in Chicago and returning to Detroit.

In time, Robin developed a successful practice as an obstetrician; the joke was he delivered half the babies in Birmingham. Betty was eager for a family of her own. Having read "Cheaper by the Dozen," she dutifully informed Robin that she wanted 10 children. In time, they settled on six – three daughters and three sons.

Betty was the parent who provided a sense of organization in a household that was chaotic. Every Sunday, she would fry bacon and scramble eggs before the entire family drove to church. She scrupulously divided everything equally among her kids, even to the point of buying one chocolate candy bar and slicing it into six pieces. To make certain everyone took their vitamins, she lined them up, instructed them to tilt their heads back and open their mouths. Then she would take a bottle of liquid vitamins and fire a squirt in every mouth. Before every Christmas, she would write down the names of the six kids and drop them into an envelope. Each would then fish one out and buy a gift for whoever's name was on the paper. That way each only had to buy one gift rather than five.

Although the three girls became best of friends as adults, like most kids they squabbled. Sue, who was 21 in January of 1965, was the oldest and Robin's favorite, although the others grumbled that she was spoiled and manipulative. Next came Ellen who was just a few months shy of 17, then Mike, who was 16, 14-year-old Nancy and the two youngest boys, Jimmy and David, who were 12 and nine respectively. Ellen and Nancy, in particular, seemed to grate on each other. Nancy thought Ellen a whiner and once threw a radio at her. There were four bedrooms upstairs and in a vain effort to keep peace, Betty shifted the girls to different rooms. The bickering between Nancy and Ellen left Betty frustrated. She blamed Nancy, whom one neighborhood mother dubbed "Nasty." What in the world is wrong with Nancy, an exasperated Betty asked Robin? He shrugged and gave a physician's answer, one typical of the era: "Perhaps she's menstruating."(22)

The three boys shared one bedroom, which Betty furnished with a pair of bunk beds, dressers and wallpaper hung by Robin and Mike. David and Jim shared one bunk bed; Mike had the other to himself. Mike kept a clock radio next to his bed, allowing him to listen to the latest rock songs on WKNR, or a Red Wings' hockey game on WWJ, often falling asleep with the radio humming.

With her take-charge personality, Betty wanted each kid to make his or her bed in the morning, although they often snuck out without doing it. Every night at 6:30, Betty served dinner, and in a typical touch of efficiency, rounded everyone up by clanging a loud bell outside the house, a shrill sound heard all over the neighborhood. Robin served, starting with David and finishing with Sue. But at that point, Robin's easy manner allowed the kids to thwart Betty's steely discipline. If they objected to Brussel sprouts or Lima beans, or complained about dinner, Robin wouldn't force the issue. But once when Nancy muttered that her pork chop looked like crap, Robin sternly dispatched her to her room. When dinner ended, Betty restored order: She designed a rigid system in which every kid knew which night was his or her turn to wash and dry the dishes. (23)

Robin would then head for the den and watch television, preferring comedy shows such as Jackie Gleason, Steve Allen and Red Skelton. The kids scattered, either out with friends, to the basement for Ping-Pong or shuffleboard or to the dining room table for homework. There was one phone upstairs for the kids to share, and its ring triggered a mad scramble.

In contrast to Betty's business-like demeanor, Robin was warmer, the parent who cuddled with kids on a couch or took them tobogganing or swimming. Once he walked into the boys' bedroom and noticed Mike listening to the Red Wings' hockey game. Robin soon treated Mike to his first Red Wings game, made even more special because they sat in front of Ted Lindsay, one of the members of the fabled 1950s Red Wing line with Gordie Howe and Sid Abel.

In the summer of 1964, Robin drove Mike and the other boys to the Upper Peninsula to fish on what Nancy called a "guys trip." (24)

Robin's office was only a couple of miles from the house, and every day he came home for lunch. Then he would take a nap on the living room couch, before waking at 1:50 p.m. to return to the office. Neither Robin nor Betty kept themselves in peak physical condition. Robin gained too much weight. Both smoked cigarettes. In 1958, when she was 42, Betty suffered a pulmonary embolism. For Nancy, the biggest shock was seeing her indomitable mother confined to bed. A few months later at age 43, Robin suffered a major heart attack. While Betty recovered, quit smoking and quickly returned to her crisp organizational style, Robin seemed different. Before the heart attack, he was eager to laugh and seemingly at ease. Now, he appeared more cynical and obsessed with death. He fretted that he would die by having a heart attack as he drove, prompting an exasperated Betty to snap, "I can walk across the street and die too." He could have quit smoking. Instead, he switched to a pipe.(25)

The year 1964 had been particularly happy for the Adairs. Sue and her longtime boyfriend became engaged. When Ellen had her 17th birthday, Betty took her and Nancy to shop in downtown Detroit at Hudson's and out to a special dinner. The family dog died, so Robin and Betty bought a second, which the kids named Ginger. Nancy and Ellen saw the Beatles at the same concert in Detroit that Nancy Henderson and Peachie Barnum attended; Nancy Adair screamed and thought John Lennon "looked so tough."(26) A wave of new films swept through the Uptown Birmingham. Mike and Nancy saw most of them–"Becket" with Peter O'Toole and Richard Burton; "Fail Safe," a nuclear disaster thriller featuring Henry Fonda as the president of the United States, and "My Fair Lady" with Audrey Hepburn.

During the last two weeks of August of 1964, Robin and Betty took the kids to vacation at Glen Lake, a shallow fresh water lake just three miles from Lake Michigan and within sight of the Sleeping Bear Dunes. When they arrived, raw temperatures and high winds transformed Glen Lake into a choppy maelstrom, making it nearly impossible to water ski. So the kids hiked about the dunes, built fires at night and toasted marshmallows. One night, Mike saw three bright lights in the black sky; he swore they were UFOs. Because it was so cold, they went to a drive-in theater to see the Beatles hit film, "A Hard Day's Night." One afternoon, Ginger gave everyone a scare by swimming so far out into Lake Michigan that the kids were alarmed she would never return. After a few days of cold weather, the temperature rose and the winds vanished, leaving Glen Lake as smooth as a pane of glass, and allowing the kids to rent paddleboards, water ski, or lounge about and get a deep sunburn. Then back to Birmingham, where Mike would enter his junior year at Seaholm. He wanted to break one minute in the backstroke, date Janice and continue a journey to become a physician. (27)

FOUR

"Your friend always, Bruce Berridge"

For more than an hour they munched on pizza and drank cokes at a table at Casa Mia. Bruce Berridge did not particularly like pizza, so he nibbled on the thick crust. As a joke, Mike ate a slice of pizza and tossed the leftover crust across the table toward Bruce who gobbled it up. They talked about driving to Susie Martin's house, which was just a short jog from Peachie's and Sandy's homes. Bruce was dating Susie and everyone liked her house because it had a recreation room for the winter and a swimming pool for the summer.

Bruce had a throbbing headache, but it would have been unthinkable for Roddy Henderson and Mike Adair to be out without Bruce. Mike and Bruce had known each other since the third grade at Quarton and the three boys made a point of standing together for the junior high varsity club photo in 1963. Bruce joined the junior high choir because Mike sang. Bruce swam on the school teams because Mike and Roddy were swimmers. He plugged away as a breaststroker and medleyist, even though he was nowhere near as fast as his two buddies. But in his dogged way, Bruce stayed with the Seaholm team even though it meant competing with the backups on the junior varsity.

Of the three boys at the table, Bruce had the most complex personality, a virtual study in contrasts. He was handsome but painfully shy around girls. He was considerate to friends, always opening a car door for a girl, but tough enough to scare off bullies. He was diligent, yet loved reckless stunts, such as tossing a cherry bomb in a neighbor's mailbox. He regarded Roddy as his best friend, but was in awe of Roddy's ability to swim so fast or earn good grades without trying. By contrast, Bruce was slavishly perfectionist.

He had pale blue eyes, a bright smile and wavy blond hair combed in the style introduced by the Beach Boys. Girls at Barnum and Seaholm described him as adorable. "Who didn't have a crush on

Bruce?" one girl recalled.(1) Yet because he was so reticent, girl after girl failed to get his attention. Linda Stubbs, who was so beautiful that she served as J-Hop queen at Seaholm, thought Bruce was "darling" and kept hoping he would ask her out. But to her chagrin, the only time Bruce noticed her was when she had a large cast wrapped around a fractured right ankle. He would thoughtfully carry her books and ask, "Hey Limpy, how are you doing?"(2) When a buddy would tip him off about a girl's interest, Bruce would shrug and say, "Oh, she's not interested in me."

Those who dated Bruce tended to be pushy, such as Martha Jean Payton, who concluded that he was too bashful to ask her out. The two went steady in junior high school and Martha Jean even coaxed a kiss from Bruce while on a hayride with other teenagers. She felt comfortable with him because he would never attempt anything other than a kiss, even though "everybody else was probably doing other things."(3) In his fashion, Bruce never was persuaded she liked him, confiding to Mike Adair that Martha Jean was "getting sick of me because we have been at most of the parties together."(4) He later dated Ellen Tower and dated Susie Martin, both of whom were self-assured.

On this cold January night at Casa Mia's, Bruce was with the people he felt most comfortable around. Except for Peachie, they all had known each other since elementary school; Sandy, Roddy and Mike were members of the same fourth-grade class, while Bruce and Sandy were in the same Seaholm homeroom class. Bruce once penned a note to Mike in a Barnum yearbook and rather than signing just his name, he inscribed, "Your friend always, Bruce Berridge." The five kids laughing at the table were the best of friends.

Bruce Berridge was lucky to be alive and eating pizza crust that night. Much like Mike, he was prone to accidents. As a kid he was clunked in the head by a tar bucket. He flipped over a go-cart when he swerved to avoid some dog waste in the middle of the road. While at the family cottage at Platte Lake near Traverse City, a buddy whacked him in the eye with a fisherman's hook and he needed stitches. One wintry afternoon in the third grade, Bruce exchanged snowballs with his older brother Jim, who retaliated by washing snow in Bruce's face. Jim dashed across the street with Bruce in hot pursuit. Bruce slipped on the icy street and a neighbor's car rolled over him, the rear tire skidding to a halt just as it seemed certain to crush Bruce's head. An ambulance rushed him to nearby Beaumont Medical Center where physicians discovered a ruptured stomach and enlarged liver. A neighborhood girl who harbored a deep crush on Bruce was so fearful he would die that she prayed for him every night. (5)

The accident, however, inexplicably helped Bruce overcome Celiac disease, a rare liver disorder that strikes just one in 333 people. As a kid, Bruce could not digest sugars, wheat, barley and rye, and suffered from chronic stomach pain. When he was two years old, his parents took him to New York City where a blood test produced the diagnosis. From then on, sweets and sugars were out. When Bruce went to birthday parties, he ate egg whites, bananas and cottage cheese. Bruce ate so many bananas that Jim was sickened at the sight of them. Virtually everyone with Celiac disease has it for life. But when physicians sewed his stomach back after the accident, Bruce's liver unexpectedly shrank to a normal size. For the first time in his life he could eat cake, ice cream and candy like any other kid.

Bruce and his brother Jim could not have been more different. Jim was supremely self-confident; Bruce was shy. Jim stood slightly over six feet in height while Bruce was 5-foot-9. Jim looked more like their mother Rita, a beautiful woman with short auburn hair who came to the United States from England when she was 10. Bruce shared his father Ken's physical appearance and dogged personality.

Bruce was not terribly serious about school at first. The family moved to Birmingham as Bruce entered the third grade at Quarton, a more advanced elementary school than his old school. Rita was not happy with his performance. So Bruce repeated the third grade, but from then on he relentlessly read the books assigned to him and always produced his homework on time. He maintained a solid B average, although he complained that he had to work hard for decent grades. He had difficulty memorizing textbook assignments, so he scrupulously read them over and over until he was sure of the content. He did not particularly like classes in English and foreign languages, but loved mathematics and science. Like Mike Adair, Bruce wanted to be a doctor and with his zealous determination and quest for perfection, he would succeed. Once he decided what he wanted to accomplish, Bruce would stubbornly persist. "No one was more focused in our group," recalled Dick Lowrie, a high school buddy.

Much like his dad, Bruce was restless and thrived on being busy. There was schoolwork, swimming, the choir, a job delivering the Detroit News and snow skiing with friends at nearby Pine Knob, although he fussed that he wasn't very good at the sport. Bruce fretted about being overweight, so he worked out and became so strong that he was known throughout Barnum for winning arm wrestling contests in a snap. Sometimes for fun, he would do a handstand and walk upside down for a few feet.(6) He was slow to anger, but nobody dared mess with Bruce Berridge; one friend swore that he could have taken Roddy apart and Roddy knew it. When a neighborhood bully called "Big John" picked on a younger kid, Bruce stepped in front and firmly said, "Leave him alone." (7)

Bruce's father Ken did not attend college, but through ingenuity and persistence launched a company that produced brake lines and windshield squirters for the auto companies. During the summer when the family vacationed at Platte Lake, Ken stayed in Birmingham to work. He was the firm's manager and its secretary. He designed the machines and served as a salesman, particularly during the slow summer months when the company sought new business for the fall. When he could find time, Ken played catch with the boys or built them a snappy metal go-cart, just like the front-engine Indianpolis-500 roadsters. The police did not like the boys driving the roadster on the street, so, naturally, Bruce and Jim defiantly raced it on the streets. They often drove to Cranbrook to watch the Detroit Lions of the National Football League conduct their August pre-season camp. Once when Jim drove Roddy to the camp, several of the Lions gathered around the roadster, with defensive tackle Alex Karras plopping down on the seat. The 260-pound Karras was so heavy he could not fit completely inside, so he left his feet dangling outside the go-cart.

During the winter, Ken escorted them to nearby Quarton Lake for an afternoon of ice skating, although as Ken demonstrated one maneuver, he tumbled backwards. Thinking their dad had performed a funny stunt, the boys burst out laughing until they realized he had fractured a rib. (8) But Ken had his own mischievous side. At Platte Lake, Bruce was irritated with the clanging sound of nearby wind chimes and decided to shut them up for good with a firecracker. But every time he struck a match, the wind blew it out. To the rescue came Ken, who skillfully lit the match and exploded the firecracker. (9)

While Bruce was shy, Ken was outgoing, perfectly at ease with friends and strangers. Bruce often thought of Ken as the "life of the party." Ken and Rita loved to entertain, with Rita playing an organ and Ken strumming a bass he designed himself: A metal bucket attached to a broom and a string.

The job of keeping the house orderly and the kids in line fell to Rita, who was a bit too naïve, almost like June Cleaver trying to handle Jim and Bruce. "She had no idea what those two were doing," one friend laughed years later.(10) With neighborhood kids dashing in and out of the house, Rita seemed like a permanent baby sitter, although she found time for her real loves–painting landscapes and playing the organ. She had help from her mother, Minnie, whom the boys loved, nicknaming her Hazel after the star of the popular TV show about a maid who was wiser than the couple she worked for. Bruce and Jim would goad her into snapping "bloody hell" in her heavy English accent. But at times, even Minnie found Bruce and Jim too much. Once when Ken and Rita arrived in Florida for a vacation, they telephoned Minnie to find out how she and the boys were doing at home. "You've got to come back because they're swinging from the drapes like monkeys," Minnie cried out.(11)

Minnie was famous for baking delicious chocolate-chip cookies, and Bruce, Roddy and Mike were just as notorious for swiping them.

So she decided to outwit them by hiding a batch in the dishwasher. Bruce, Mike and Roddy stormed about the house in search of the cookies. Where were they, they kept demanding? Then she made the mistake of walking into the breezeway that linked the house to the garage. Bruce locked the door and would not let her in until she told him where the cookies were. She refused and waited in the breezeway bench until the boys finally looked in the dishwasher. (12)

Bruce grew up in a home designed and built by Ken in the nearby suburb of Franklin, a more remote and wooded area than Birmingham. Bruce and Jim shared a bedroom, but they loved the spacious backyard, which allowed them to sled every winter. When Bruce was 7, the family moved to a roomier two-story brick home on Westwood in Birmingham, which once had been the home of Democratic U.S. Senator Phil Hart. It had a spacious front yard shaded by a large elm. The house had a large living room with a bay window and a fireplace. Ken entertained friends in the living room with his homemade bass. There was a library off to the right where Jim and Bruce studied in the afternoon. In the evening, Ken and Rita, smoking her ever-present Parliaments, slipped into the library to watch Jackie Gleason, Perry Como, Ozzie and Harriet and Jack Benny on a new color RCA. The first-floor breezeway led to what had originally been a maid's room. For the boys, it was a perfect TV room where they could turn up the volume or make as much noise as they wished. A U-shaped staircase illuminated by a tall window led to four bedrooms upstairs, one of which served as a spare for guests. Jim and Bruce had separate bedrooms in back with a connecting bathroom. In the basement, the boys had a Lionel train on oval-shaped train tracks. Quickly bored with watching the train race by in the same circle, they pleaded with Ken and Rita to buy them a more elaborate track. When their parents refused, the boys announced they would rather pack up the old train set.

Bruce and Jim were such a combustible pair that Bruce joked his father "could have wrung our necks." More often than not, Jim was the instigator and Bruce the tag along. They swiped wood from nearby homebuilding sites and constructed their own stagecoach.

They built an elaborate tree fort connected to the house. When they were finished, they decided the wood needed aging. They could have stained it, but Jim thought it would be faster to douse it with gasoline and set it afire. Although they ran the risk of burning down the house, Jim waited until the wood was properly charred and then put out the fire.

They fired BB guns at wasp nests and dashed away to escape the wrath of the angry insects. When that was not thrilling enough, they crept closer to the nests and sprayed them with Raid, despite Rita's admonition not "to go back there to the wasp nests." They stole hatpins from their mother's wardrobe, inserted them into peashooters and fired away. They shot arrows from bows, with Bruce once hitting Jim in the arm. They loved to play a game called Mumbletypeg, where they balanced a knife on the tip of their fingers and flipped it in the air with the hope of getting it stuck in the ground, although Bruce more often than not ended up with the knife stuck into one of his arms. At night, Bruce and Jim climbed out their bedroom windows, plopped down on large Frisbees and slid down the roof, catching themselves at the gutter. If they missed the gutter, they tumbled the eight feet to the ground, but because the grass was soft, neither ever broke a bone. Once Bruce tried to break his fall by grasping a pine tree, but he fell to the ground when the top of the tree broke. (13)

At Platte Lake, Bruce and a buddy amused themselves by blowing up a neighbor's mailbox. With assembly-line precision, the friend opened the mailbox lid, Bruce tossed a cherry bomb inside, shut the lid and nonchalantly walked away. The muffled explosion blew the lid open, prompting the angry neighbor to demand that a police officer find the culprit. The officer rounded up every kid he could find, ordered them to stand in line and pronounced, "Whoever didn't do it, step back." As most of the kids stepped back, Bruce and his buddy were honest enough to stand still, thus implicating themselves.

Bruce met Roddy after the family moved to Westwood and the two hit it off immediately. Roddy had a clubhouse behind the garage of the old Glenhurst house where he and Bruce watched TV. Roddy often invited friends over for a basement party to blast records. Helen Henderson fixed sandwiches, although Bruce found it amusing that she painstakingly trimmed the crust from the bread for Roddy and his sister Nancy.

During the winter, Roddy and Bruce biked to a nearby lake and made their way across the ice to a small island. Sometimes the ice broke and they tumbled into the frigid water, but because it was only knee deep they did not get too wet. Then the two grilled hamburgers on improvised stoves known as buddy burners–placing a sterno inside coffee cans and frying the hamburgers on top. (14) In the spring, Bruce, Roddy and Mike biked to Cranbrook, the exclusive private school where they raced their bikes against the sloped slate-colored walls of a man-made pond called Big Jonah, which was shaded by rows of pine trees. The boys boldly capped off the experience by riding straight into the water, sometimes daring each other to fly over the handlebars and land in the pond. They played ice hockey at a friend's house, although when Bruce's brother Jim played goalie he lost a tooth from being hit with a puck. During the sixth and seventh grades, they spent hours every afternoon jumping on Ellen Tower's trampoline; Bruce was sure that Roddy's skill as a diver was in part the result of the time spent on that trampoline.(15)

Roddy's willingness to take risks brought out Bruce's reckless side. On New Year's Eve in 1963, they tossed a cherry bomb into a neighbor's mailbox, a repeat of Bruce's stunt at Platte Lake. The bomb exploded in spectacular fashion, but neither boy noticed a nearby police car. They were taken to the Birmingham police station where their mortified parents had to fetch them.

On Halloween night in 1964, Bruce, Roddy and Mike concocted an elaborate plan to catch younger kids who were soaping the windows of darkened homes. With Roddy's parents out for the evening, they gathered at the Henderson house, switched off the lights and hid in the living room. When kids failed to show up, the perplexed boys decided a pumpkin on the front door might attract them. So Roddy swiped a well-lit pumpkin off a neighbor's porch and placed it near the Henderson front door. All of a sudden, the irritated neighbor stormed into the Henderson house in search of his pumpkin, forcing Bruce, Roddy and Mike to scatter upstairs and hide in the bathrooms.(16)

As junior high swimmers they were ineligible to compete in a state meet, but they could certainly dream about it. They attended the senior high state championship, held in alternating years at either the University of Michigan or Michigan State University. As a treat, Eddie Watkins' father would drive Roddy, Mike, Bruce and Eddie to the meet, take a motel room for himself and pack the four boys in a second room. They would watch the preliminary heats on Friday night, but that was just the beginning of their fun. Back at the motel room, they stayed up most of the night, practicing their racing dives by leaping from a chair into the bed, which created a deafening noise. The next morning as they chowed down at breakfast, they heard people complain about having noisy neighbors. Then it was off to the pool for the state finals before the return trip to Birmingham. (17)

Bruce may have been in awe of Roddy and his self-assured personality, but he didn't emulate his buddy's style. Bruce never would have written the boastful type of yearbook note that Roddy scribbled to one girl who had a penchant for pretending she was dumb. "You know what?" Roddy wrote. "You're a perfect girl except for one thing. You're too dumb! You just gotta get smarter! Maybe someday you can be as smart as I am. But it's going to take a lot of work." Instead, in a note a couple years earlier to the same girl, Bruce wrote, "I wish that I had seen you more this year. I am glad that you're treas."–a reference to her being elected student council treasurer. (18)

Bruce developed a close friendship with Bill Saefkow, who lived just across the street. Saefkow weighed no more than 105 pounds, suffered from asthma, and was one grade behind Bruce who was in the 11th grade. Roddy wanted nothing to do with a 10th grade boy, but Bruce liked Saefkow, who in turn regarded Bruce as a big brother. Bruce was fascinated by Saefkow's elaborate collection of stamps. Someday, Bruce would say, he would start his own collection. (19)

Summer was Bruce's favorite season because it meant days at Platte Lake. As soon as the school year ended, the Berridges headed north to the glassy smooth fresh-water lake tucked like a large spoon in the tree-covered hills near Traverse City and the coast of Lake Michigan. Ken and Rita owned a cottage on the lake's southwest corner, next to similar homes owned by Bruce's cousin and aunt. The lake was so remote the Berridges would drive U.S. 10 through Saginaw, Flint and Clare–a six-hour trip before the opening of Interstate 75 in the 1960s. A tiny dirt road completed the journey to the cottage, which was shaded by evergreens, birch and maple trees. The two-story home had two bedrooms, living room, dining room, an open-air porch furnished with wicker, and a bathroom. Before the Berridges installed a shower in the bathroom, Bruce and Jim cleaned up every morning by leaping into the lake.

From the back of the house, the ground sloped down toward the lake and a long dock, where the Berridges moored a rowboat powered by a five-horsepower Johnson outboard engine that propelled the craft through the water at five miles per hour. Ken used the powered rowboat to take Bruce and Jim down the river that linked Platte Lake with Lake Michigan. From then on, the two boys were confident enough to make the trip on their own.

Because the wind blew from the southwest, Platte Lake was calm, ideal for jumping the wake while water skiing. The rowboat was too poky to haul a skier, so Bruce and Jim bought gasoline for a friend who would let them water ski behind his 40-horsepower boat. During the afternoons, they skied, swam and slept on the beach, working up rich tans. They built a series of forts, with the most elaborate a three-story beauty. That one nearly got them into trouble when a local police officer demanded to know where they got all the new wood. Do we have to tell you in front of our father, the boys asked? When the officer nodded, they led him into the garage and pointed to the rafters where they had removed the boards. "Your problem now," the officer jokingly told Ken Berridge, who ordered the boys to dismantle the fort. (20)

Dissatisfied with the slow rowboat, Bruce and Jim built speedy hydroplanes. They started with a four-by-eight foot sheet of marine plywood, sliced a groove up the center for 18 inches and molded the two ends into the bow of a small boat. Then they constructed a top and sides, attached a five-horsepower Johnson outboard, and in two days had a new boat capable of cruising the lake at 22 miles per hour. When that was not fast enough, Bruce and Jim built a larger boat and installed a 20-horsepower Mercury engine, which allowed the craft to zip through the water at 36 miles per hour. They particularly enjoyed steering the boats up the Platte River to Lake Michigan, although rules of the river prohibited boats creating large wakes or going faster than five miles per hour. That may have been fine for small rowboats, but it posed a dilemma for the hydroplanes. If Bruce and Jim obeyed both rules, their boat would scrape the bottom. To stay off the bottom, they needed to go five miles per hour, but at that slow speed they left a choppy wake. The only way to eliminate the wake was to go faster than the speed limit. Given the choice, they opted to break the speed law.

There was little to do at night, because the black-and-white television set could pick up only one channel in Traverse City and sometimes that signal was too fuzzy to watch. The radio was just as useless, catching the signal of only one local station. Every so often, they drove into nearby Frankfort or Beulah for a film. When Mike Adair was visiting, they would pile five kids into a car and sneak two more into the trunk to get them in free of charge at the Cherry Bowl drive-in. When they were younger, Bruce, Jim and the handful of kids around the lake played hide-and-seek before gathering around the dining room table for Hearts or Cribbage. The real boredom set in when it rained. During one rainstorm, Rita thought it would be useful to teach the boys how to weave baskets, an idea that Jim thought was appalling.

A fireplace supplied the cottage's heat, which meant by Labor Day with its chilly temperatures, the Berridges returned to Birmingham.

In many ways, September was starting fresh for Bruce. Cut off from most radio and television during the summer, Bruce had no idea about the new rock songs or TV hits. So Roddy and Mike had to fill him in on the latest fads. The three attended Friday night football games at Seaholm, chowed down hamburgers at Ted's and Maverick's and rode with Roddy in his mother's Skylark. Every school morning, they scrambled into Ken's car for the short drive to Seaholm. Because it was early in the morning, they usually slouched half-asleep into the seats, although one time Ken woke them with the cry of, "You dumb shit!" Another car had cut him off. Bruce took more advanced chemistry and biology classes and even enjoyed an English class in the 10th grade, in part because Roddy and Mike were in the same class, but also because Bruce and his friends thought the teacher was so effective.(21)

Seaholm was more grueling for Bruce than junior high. Because Roddy and Mike were on the varsity swimming team, they worked out after school and headed for home at a reasonable hour. By contrast, Bruce practiced later in the evening with the junior varsity, having only started serious swimming in the 7th grade. The exercise was good, but Bruce knew he lacked the motivation to dedicate himself to swimming the entire year. Because they were athletes, they did not smoke cigarettes, as many Seaholm students did. They also shunned beer, largely because one of Bruce's friends drank too much one night and had his stomach pumped.

As sensitive as Bruce was, he could not help but notice in the 11th grade that Roddy was spending more time with Dave Nelson, one of the very few people that Roddy ever looked up to. Roddy seemed in awe of Nelson, who knew so much about surfing from his days living in California. Such worries said more about Bruce than Roddy, because as one friend said, "He knew Roddy and he had Roddy's number."(22)

On weekends, Bruce was content to let Roddy drive. Unlike Roddy, Bruce was not eager to drive. He seemed nervous driving, in part because cars had caused him so much grief. Not only was he run over by a car in the third grade, but his brother Jim was in a jeep when it flipped over at Platte Lake. Jim once rounded up a police car's flashing light and slapped it on top of the family car. Then Jim and Bruce raced around the small roads near the lake and turned on the police light to give unsuspecting motorists a good scare. It all seemed like fun until one day near Crystal Mountain Jim swerved to avoid an oncoming car and slammed into a truck. Bruce, sitting in the back seat, was only shaken, but the car took a beating.

Hours before the Saturday afternoon Central swim meet, Bruce darted across the street to see Bill Saefkow. For an hour, they pored through Saefkow's stamp collection. As he got up to leave, Bruce mentioned plans for the late-night pizza. "Do you want to go?" Saefkow hesitated. It sounded like fun. His parents were out for the night and except for his younger sister, the house was empty. But Saefkow shook his head. He knew Roddy and Mike would not want a 10th grade boy hanging around with them. Shortly before 3 in the afternoon, Bruce left the Saefkow house and dashed through the snow and across the street to his house.(23)

FIVE

"At home in a car"

Just after 10 p.m., they left the comfortable warmth of the pizza parlor for the bitter cold outdoors. Roddy Henderson jumped into the Skylark's front seat with Peachie Barnum taking her customary perch next to him. Mike Adair claimed the coveted shotgun seat, while Sandy Christman and Bruce Berridge edged into the back, with Sandy directly behind Roddy. The Skylark had lap seat belts, but none of the kids buckled them.

Roddy edged the Skylark out onto Woodward; its eight lanes clear of snow and ice. He steered into the left lane past the intersection of 14-Mile Road until he approached a fork where the business route of Woodward branched left through uptown Birmingham and the right swept around the eastern edge of uptown. Roddy took the business route of Woodward into uptown. It was 10:17 p.m.

In the darkened back seat, Bruce and Sandy chattered away over the sound of rock songs from the AM radio. Just back from a family vacation in Mexico, Sandy Christman sported a deep bronze tan from hours of water skiing and scuba diving. She had returned with gifts for a handful of friends, presenting Betsy Brenton with a round, silver charm for a necklace.(1) Sandy had been so busy lately that she fretted about not spending time with longtime friends. Just the day before the Central meet as the students shivered outside during a fire drill, Sandy promised a close friend to "do things more often."(2)

Sandy Christman's passion was sports. She was a physically strong and agile athlete–game for tennis, snow skiing, field hockey and water skiing. As an elementary school student, Sandy hung out with like-minded girls who jokingly referred to themselves as tomboys and hoped to be the first women to play major league baseball for the Detroit Tigers. If Roddy, Bruce and the other guys were playing sports, they wanted in. There was dodge ball with the guys who wanted Sandy on their team because she was so good. They played touch football in a neighbor's yard. There was baseball–both hardball and softball–over at the elementary school. Sandy was so adept at softball that she threw the ball exactly as a boy did. She and her friends were particularly irritated when the boys left them behind for one of their organized school sports, a fact of life in 1965 that struck them as unfair. Had Sandy grown up in a later era, she would have won a college scholarship to swim or play softball and field hockey.(3)

After her father assembled a go-cart powered by an old lawn mower engine, Sandy and her friends spent hours zipping up the neighborhood sidewalks. Then they would pack a picnic lunch, hop on their bikes and dash over to an empty field.(4) Because Roddy and Dave Nelson built bunboards, so did Sandy, who was so daring that she once fractured an ankle during a spill. When one of her girlfriends asked for help in building her own board, Sandy told her, "I'll make it for you." She took her friend's roller skates and skillfully attached them to a smooth board.(5) During the winter, Sandy snow skied, preferring the hills at Otsego or the Colorado mountains on family trips. The Christmans loved to snow ski; Sandy's mother Vicki once broke a leg skiing in the Alps. When Derby Junior High School formed a ski club in 1963 while Sandy was in the ninth grade, she and her newest friend Peachie Barnum promptly joined. Every Thursday afternoon they changed into warmer clothes and jackets, grabbed their snow skis and boarded a yellow school bus for the 45-minute drive to Mt. Holly, where they skied until evening.

When Jack Barnum moved his family across the triangle from the Christmans in 1961, Sandy and Peachie became "inseparable friends" even though they could not have been more different. (6) Sandy was tall, willowy and buff, towering a good five inches over Peachie. While Peachie flawlessly groomed her curly blonde hair and wore the latest style of clothes, Sandy never really fussed with her silky, dishwater blonde hair, often tying it back in a haphazard ponytail. In 9th grade, she cropped it as short as the boys. She wore skirts to school because the dress code required them, but preferred to flop around in slacks or shorts. Unlike other girls who would duck into the restrooms to apply makeup, Sandy could have cared less, and where Peachie loved the talent shows at Derby, Sandy was notably unenthusiastic.

Friends joked that Sandy and Peachie "sort of balanced each other out."(7) Sandy's friends tended to be athletic or very serious. Some confused Sandy's quiet demeanor with shyness. They were wrong. Sandy Christman had an infectious laugh and a dry sense of humor. When Mike Adair or another friend would say something silly, Sandy would respond with a half-smile. She once pasted into a friend's yearbook a small cartoon of two people napping as they propped their feet up on a coffee table. The caption read, "Next week we've got to get organized." She then wrote her own name next to one of the cartoon characters and her friend's name next to the other, adding, "Lots of luck, Sandy."(8)

Peachie sparked a responsive chord in Sandy. Around Peachie "she wasn't so quiet."(9) The two spent winter performing water ballet at Derby, summer at the Birmingham Country Club, and autumn in East Lansing for tailgate parties before Michigan State football games.

While Peachie enjoyed swimming and diving, she did not have the same zeal for the sport as Sandy did. They joined the country club's swimming team, and Sandy quickly excelled at the rigorous workouts. She became the club's best at the butterfly and was so skilled at every stroke that she seemed certain to swim the individual medley for local American Athletic Union clubs. She was just as intense about water ballet. Sandy and Peachie would arrive shortly after six in the morning and perform the water ballet routines and, on occasion, work out with the boys' swimming team. Her passion for sports was reflected in a brief yearbook note she scribbled to a water-ballet teammate in the eighth grade: "To a real cute girl who is a terrific swimmer." A year later, as Sandy was leaving Derby for Seaholm, she could barely contain her excitement about swimming for Corey Van Fleet's AAU team, known as the Maple Swim Club. AAU swimming was one of the few sports where boys and girls could participate. It included a grueling schedule of late-evening workouts, followed by weekend meets. "Nancy, it's been fun knowing you and swimming with you," Sandy wrote in a friend's ninth-grade yearbook. "I might see you at the Maples before the year (summer) is over. Good luck. Love 'ya, Sandy." (10)

Sandy towered over many of the boys in junior high, and did not date much. By the time she entered the eleventh grade, her father noticed "she was just starting to show an interest in boys." (11) Just as in athletics, she showed an assertive style toward guys, even asking one boy in her art class to join her on a date. (12)

At 17, she was the oldest of four kids. Her sister Donna was 15, Linda was 13, and Tom, the youngest, was 11. Krisa Barnum often played with Tom and Linda, whom Krisa idolized because she had the best Barbie collection in the neighborhood. When Krisa was with Tom, their mischievous sides came out. They hid behind the hedges and lobbed dirt balls at passing cars. Every day at the Christman house seemed like fun.

Sandy's father Dale was an osteopathic surgeon and just about everyone called him Dr. Dale. With his powerful chest and stocky build, the 44-year old Dr. Dale looked more like an offensive tackle than a skilled physician. Like Jack Barnum, Dr. Dale grew up in Ohio, where his father Louis was a famous aircraft designer in Dayton. When Orville Wright and Colonel Edward Andrew Deeds, one of the original founders of Delco batteries, wanted to reconstruct the original plane that flew at Kitty Hawk, they turned to Louis Christman. The replica on display at Carillon Historical Park in Dayton is Louis Christman's design. Dale Christman gravitated toward medicine. After graduating from Miami University, tucked between Cincinnati and Dayton, he attended medical school in Philadelphia. He interned in 1944 at Art Centre Hospital in Detroit and practiced there all his life, moving into Birmingham in 1953.

In the close-knit Cranbrook Yarmouth Cultural Society, Dr. Dale served as the emergency physician, once removing the tonsils of two neighborhood boys in the same day. When one of the neighbor's daughters cut her head skiing, Dr. Dale sat her down at the dining room table, told her to bite on a pencil and stitched her up.(13) The neighborhood girls liked him, although one time he inadvertently threw a scare into them. Sandy had arranged to host a slumber party and by 11 in the evening, the restless girls decided to watch a horror film on local TV. At a particularly frightening moment, Dr. Dale, home from a long day of work, opened the door and the girls shrieked in terror.(14)

He was close friends with Jack Barnum, another Miami of Ohio graduate. They partied and played bridge together and often were seen at the Birmingham Country Club, although Dr. Dale loved golf more than Jack. Just about every summer evening, Dr. Dale and another friend tried to get in as many holes as possible until dark. The caddies nicknamed them the "Night fighters." Dr. Dale was a particular favorite because he was a generous tipper.(15) During the winter, Dr. Dale and his golfing friend gathered their families together for golf trips to Florida, Puerto Rico and Palm Springs. One Christmas, the Boyles, who lived down the street, took a vacation in Aspen. While they were away, Jack and Dr. Dale gathered a group of friends, helped themselves to the Boyles' house and threw a big neighborhood party. In a playful gesture, they set up large photos of the Boyles on the front porch so everybody could pretend they were there.(16)

On this particular January evening in 1965, Dr. Dale was glad Sandy was going out to have fun with her best friends.

Someone else was out that night. Mike Drothler was driving his black 1961 Ford Galaxie convertible with white-wall tires. Ted Blakeslee, who liked to keep tabs on every snappy car in Birmingham, thought the Galaxie was one of the sharpest he had ever seen. But then, Mike Drothler lived for his cars. One year in the middle of winter, he drove a buddy back to school at Central Michigan University. In the biting cold, Mike insisted on keeping the Galaxie's top down. He simply turned up the heat. As a high school student in the suburbs of Pittsburgh, he first owned a 1953 Ford, replacing the automatic transmission with a standard shift. Under his senior class picture in the 1960 Brentwood High School yearbook, the editors wrote: "At home in a car." (17)

Mike was 22 in 1965, but was more of a throwback to the 1950s than Roddy and his friends. He collected mounds of 45s recorded by Elvis Presley, and played and replayed "Hound Dog" and "Don't Be Cruel." He combed his light brown hair into what kids in 1960 called a "Duck's Tail." One friend thought he resembled Edward Byrnes, the heartthrob star on "77 Sunset Strip," whose character "Kookie" relentlessly combed his hair. Mike was confident, "did what he wanted to do," one friend said, and was so "cool" that friends called him the "Beau Brummell of Brentwood High."(18)

Mike had always been popular. "I don't think anybody disliked him, although a lot were jealous because he was a really good looking guy," said one close friend from high school. He was handsome and he knew it. For his final two years of high school, Mike dated Liz Hemlinger, a classmate with short hair and a warm smile. Before Mike had a car, he walked Liz home from school everyday. As a junior, he played football, and she was a majorette. They went to the prom together. On weekends, he would drive her up and down Route 51, which ran through the heart of Brentwood. They were together so much that everyone, including Liz, assumed they would get married. But after the Drothlers moved to Birmingham in 1960, the relationship ended, the distance between Pennsylvania and Michigan too great to sustain a serious romance. Mike's friends said he was distraught about the break-up, although Liz later said, "He broke my heart, that's for sure."(19)

Mike had been a solid high school student. His younger brother Bob thought Mike was the smarter of the two and could pass his courses with minimal effort. By contrast, Bob felt he had to work harder than Mike to get good grades. Although Mike played football and baseball, Bob was the better athlete. After the move to Birmingham, Bob was an outstanding halfback on the Seaholm football team, starting as a junior and scoring 11 touchdowns as a senior. Bob co-captained the track team and was a member of the Varsity Club. (20)

Mike came from a family that personified the American Dream, not unlike the Barnums and Hendersons. Fred and Dorothy

Drothler, whom friends called Dottie, were hard-working parents who rose from modest backgrounds to attend college and become successful enough to live in a place like Birmingham. Fred was the second oldest of seven children. His father ran a dry cleaning shop in Harrisburg, Pennsylvania. Fred worked his way through Penn State University–the only one in his family to earn a degree–before landing a job with the Retail Credit Company, which now is Equifax. From then it was a series of promotions and constant moves. They moved so often that they rented homes instead of buying their own. But after the transfer to Michigan, Fred bought a home on Fairway Drive in Birmingham. (21)

Dottie, who grew up in Allentown, Pennsylvania, had earned a degree from a state teacher's college in Harrisburg and found a job as a teacher. But after marrying Fred, she quit and, like most women of that era, devoted her time to raising her kids. Ironically, given Mike's love for cars, Dottie refused to drive. When she first earned her license, she was involved in a car accident, slamming her head into the windshield. She was so frightened by the experience, she chose never to drive again. Instead, she would sit in the passenger seat and scrupulously watch other cars and trucks. "I'm driving every time we're in the car, but I'm driving on the passenger side," she said. "I'm looking ahead the whole time."(22)

By 1964, Fred was promoted and transferred once again–this time to New York City where he was division manager for Retail Credit's New York office. Bob was off to Bowling Green State University in northwest Ohio, his education partly financed by a $1,500 loan from his father. Mike and a buddy found an apartment in nearby Royal Oak. Michigan was now Mike's home.(23)

On the Saturday of the swimming meet, Mike Drothler worked his regular job as assistant produce manager at a nearby Kroger's. He had long been interested in running a grocery store. As a senior at Brentwood High School, Mike gave up football and instead worked after school in the produce department of a grocery store to earn enough money to buy a better car. After the move to Michigan, Mike enrolled in a management-training program sponsored by Kroger and Western Michigan University.

Even though he was just a young man, Mike had already beaten the odds twice, surviving a serious birth defect and a terrible car wreck. When Mike was an infant, nobody thought he would live for very long. He was born with aortic stenosis, which is a narrowing or obstruction of the heart's aortic valve. Because the valve could not open properly, blood did not flow throughout his body and often backed up in his lungs. Physicians told Fred and Dottie that unless surgeons could perfect an operation, Mike would not live past his early 20s. As a young boy, Mike, who was called Mickey after baseball star Mickey Mantle, could not run or swim or play baseball. On the few occasions when he did run, his face turned blue and he nearly passed out. He kept himself busy by building an elaborate set of tracks for his Lionel trains or collecting stamps. (24)

By the mid-1950s, surgeons at the University of Pittsburgh had made advances on valve surgery and they operated on the teenage Mike. After the surgery, he could play football and had every reason to live a normal life. But having been granted a reprieve, Mike seemed determined to make up for all the time he had lost as a kid. He enjoyed taking a few risks. As a high school student, he drank a beer or two on weekends, although his brother Bob later said he could not recall Mike drinking while driving.(25)

After the move to Michigan, Mike drove a 1955 Chevy, which he liked to race well above the speed limit. "He always drove fast," one friend recalled. "He was a hot rod driver." Twice he was ticketed for speeding. Once when Jay Hengelmann, a neighbor of Mike's, was home in Birmingham, Mike honked his horn to summon his friend. As Hengelmann climbed into the car, Mike handed him a Budweiser and off they went. (26)

One icy December evening in 1961, Mike joined Jay and his parents for a hockey game. After the game, Mike dropped off Jay's parents at their house. It was not yet midnight, so Mike and Jay announced they wanted to go out and get a hamburger. "Just be careful and drive safely," Kay Hengelmann told them. Off they went, downing a few beers before racing the Chevy 90 miles an hour up Maple toward Birmingham. As it passed Lake Park, the Chevy rammed a utility pole, toppled it and dragged it down the street until smacking into a second pole. The car was nearly ripped into two pieces, but amazingly, Mike and Jay were shipped to Beaumont Hospital with only concussions, cuts and bruises. When Kay Hengelmann saw her battered son at the hospital, she turned to a couple of his friends. "OK guys, I want you to take a good look. This is what happens when alcohol is involved in driving. Don't ever do it."(27) A week later, Mike and Jay were released from the hospital. Police displayed the twisted Chevy at one of the city's gas stations, hoping to discourage kids from driving while drinking. That crash, as well as others near that corner, so alarmed a Birmingham city commissioner that he asked whether the speed limit on Maple between Southfield and Cranbrook should be reduced from 35 miles an hour to 25. The commissioner grumbled that drivers only obeyed the speed limit when police cars were nearby, prompting the mayor to reply, "I think that's true with any street." The speed limit remained 35.(28)

For Jay Hengelmann, the 1961 crash was enough to convince him that drinking a few beers and driving a car were simply too dangerous. "You think you're OK and you're not," he said years later.

As Roddy and his teammates were swimming against Central late that afternoon, Mike Drothler bought six steaks and two cases of Pabst Blue Ribbon at a grocery store, explaining to a friend's mother that he planned on a big barbecue. He placed the steaks and beer in the back seat of the black Galaxie. It was so bitterly cold, that Mike kept the convertible top up. (29)

Sometime after 10 p.m., Mike was driving alone in the black Galaxie. He turned east on Maple and headed in the same direction he had taken in 1961 when he crashed his Chevy. At 75 miles per hour, he roared toward uptown Birmingham.(30)

SIX

"We've got a bunch of kids in this car."

At 10:20 p.m., the Skylark glided past the low-rise buildings uptown, the movie theater with its tall "Birmingham" sign and the twinkling lights of the White Tower hamburger stand, with a handful of late-night customers. Then it arrived at the intersection of Woodward and Maple, with Cunningham's Drug Store on the right and Lake's Jewelry store on the left. Roddy turned left on Maple.

Although Maple had four lanes, the lane nearest the curb on both sides was reserved for parallel-parking. On a typical weekday afternoon, parked cars created a traffic jam. But on this Saturday night, the only other car on Maple was an Oldsmobile driven by Ray Raupp, his wife, and their 16-year-old son Tom. They were returning from dinner and fell in behind the Skylark.(1)

Roddy drove the Skylark past Pierce, within sight of the game store owned by Susie Martin's father and the lingerie shop he called the boner store. He continued beyond Machus, a cafeteria-style restaurant on the right, and Kresge's on the left, where so often they gathered at the soda fountain. Then past Bates Street and St. James Episcopal Church on the left, while on the right the dimly lit windows of Jacobson's department store showed mannequins wearing the latest women's fashions.

It was a typical Saturday night in Birmingham. Mike's parents, Betty and Robin Adair were enjoying a casual dinner and a game of bridge with five other couples at the Bloomfield Village home of Betty's brother, Fritz Adams. The players included three physicians, a lawyer and two peddlers, one guest's joking term for salesmen. They had come of age together after the men returned from World War II, buying small $9,000 homes on Washington Boulevard or Bates Street. Now two decades later, they had prospered, moved to roomy colonials near Cranbrook with expansive yards for their kids and access to some of the finest schools in Michigan.

Jack and Betty Barnum were playing bridge with neighbors near their house. Ed and Helen Henderson opted for a quieter evening at home with Nancy. They chose to watch NBC's Saturday Night at the Movies featuring "The Swan," the final Hollywood film for actress Grace Kelly before her marriage to Prince Rainier of Monaco. Just down the street, Bill Saefkow lounged on his parents' upstairs bed and watched the same film on a small black-and-white Zenith. He kept thinking it was a silly plot. (2)

Like Roddy, Tom Lawton was in no mood to celebrate after their afternoon loss. He could have sulked and watched television. But they only had five channels to choose from, and nothing seemed particularly interesting for teenagers. WXYZ-TV had Lawrence Welk and his bubbles at 8:30 p.m. At 9:30, Bing Crosby hosted the Hollywood Palace, featuring Cyd Charisse, Bette Davis, Phil Harris, Groucho Marx and George Burns, while WJBK at 10 p.m. offered Gunsmoke. Clearly, "nobody wanted to go home and watch TV with their parents." So Lawton borrowed the family car, collected a few swimming buddies and drove uptown in search of a snack. (3)

Betsy Brenton and her friend already were at the Birmingham Theater where they bought tickets to watch Susan Hayward and Bette Davis in "Where Love Has Gone." Carol Wollenberg had taken an overnight bag on her double date so she could spend the night at her girlfriend's. Sandy Christman's close friend Sandy Clemens was on a date. Mike Adair's cousin, Bob Adams, escaped the bridge game at his parent's house and was making out with a date in a friend's basement. He couldn't wait to tell his cousin.

Ellen Adair watched TV at her house with a boyfriend she was thinking of breaking up with. Her two younger brothers slept upstairs. Nancy Adair was at a surprise party for a friend, annoyed when a guy she liked made out with a friend of hers.

Janice Poplack, the girl Mike Adair asked out, baby-sat for her younger brother at their home on Lake Park. Nancy Ackerly, a close friend of Mike and Bruce, was at her parents' house at the corner of

Westwood and Maple. Dave Nelson was also home, but was so sick from the flu that he was sleeping. Corey Van Fleet had left Seaholm shortly after 4:30 p.m., taking just enough time to tidy up the pool, remove the lane markers and lock the door. He drove the short distance to his home in Southfield.

In the sun parlor of his home at the corner of Aspen and Maple, 14-year-old Jim McGowan watched television, the sound interrupted by cars driving on Maple. In the very next house, Bob Lyndall, a 17-year-old Seaholm junior, watched a National Hockey League game and debated whether to check out the latest issue of Playboy. Next door, John Schaeffer, a 15-year-old Seaholm sophomore, had the house to himself. His father, a physician, and his mother were down the street playing bridge with friends. So he turned on the latest rock songs and chatted on the phone with his best friend, Alex Grether—the same boy who had watched Roddy swim for the first time that afternoon. Alex lived one street over on Linden.

Patrolman Herb Duncan of the Birmingham police was near the end of a routine evening, much like every night in a town where serious crime was rare. He filled his car with gasoline and was "killing some time" by driving west on Maple. (4)

At Michigan State University in East Lansing, most students were partying or, like Jacquey Barnum, on a date. Her younger sister Patty was at a party with a Michigan State quarterback. A friend poured Patty a glass of vodka. She took a sip, her first drink of hard liquor. Patty didn't like the taste, so she poured the rest into the pot of an artificial tree. Seeing the empty glass, the friend poured more vodka. Once again, Patty took a quick sip and tossed the remainder away. Bruce Berridge's brother Jim, a Michigan State junior, laughed away the night with his fraternity buddies at Phi Kappa Phi. Jim Henderson was trying without success to have fun at another fraternity party. Normally he would have, but on this particular evening, he felt depressed. He barely talked with his blind date as he sipped a beer. He never felt so odd. (5)

By now, the Skylark had cleared uptown Birmingham. From now on, street parking was prohibited, opening up all four lanes to cars and creating more room to maneuver. Plows had piled mountains of snow and ice on either side of Maple, the white peaks illuminated by the streetlights. Strong winds blew specks of snow across the street, but the road was dry. The temperature had fallen to 9 degrees. Roddy carefully drove no faster than 35 miles per hour. The radio blared out the latest rock hits.(6)

The Skylark and Oldsmobile passed the light at Southfield Road. Roddy steered into the left lane while Ray Raupp hugged the right lane just two lengths behind, the Skylark's red rear lights clearly visible. Just behind them was Officer Duncan, although he was far enough back that he could not see either car. The Skylark and Raupp's Oldsmobile headed down into a small valley and across the bridge that spanned the Rouge River. During the day, drivers had a panoramic view of the waterfalls and Quarton Lake on the right, but now night concealed the lake from Roddy's view. Then up a slight hill past Aspen where Jim McGowan watched TV and John Schaeffer chatted on the phone with Alex Grether. In a moment, they would drive by Alex's house on Linden on the left. Another mile and Roddy would reach Cranbrook and the turn to Susie Martin's house. It was 10:22 p.m.

From the opposite direction, the black Galaxie convertible zipped past three young hitchhikers. They followed the Galaxie as it wove through the intersection of Maple and Cranbrook and past the First Presbyterian Church and the First United Methodist Church, a handsome brick structure of Tudor design. Lake Park loomed ahead on the left. Just past Lake Park, Maple veered to the right, the same bend Mike Drothler missed three and one-half years ago with his 1955 Chevy.(7)

It was 10:23 p.m.

From the Oldsmobile's back seat, Tom Raupp saw a flash of white headlights. In the Skylark, Bruce Berridge may have had time to shout, "Oh God, no!" There was no sound of screeching brakes but a booming explosion so loud that Nancy Ackerly heard it from her house nearly a mile away. To Jim McGowan, it was earsplitting. Alex Grether was sure someone heaved a cherry bomb into his front yard. The black Galaxie rammed Roddy's side of the Skylark and created a flash of yellow sparks. One case of long-necked Pabst Blue Ribbon beer bottles ripped through the plastic canvas of the convertible's back window. Mike Adair smacked his head into the front windshield and a radio knob on the dashboard. Bruce Berridge slammed into the front seat, and as the right door sprung open, Bruce was ejected onto the pavement curb. The black Galaxie shoved the Skylark into the Oldsmobile, which skidded to a stop against a telephone pole. Roddy's car careened to a halt in front of a large oak tree near the waterfalls, 60 feet from the black Galaxie. The Skylark and Galaxie lay motionless and parallel to each other. The street was littered with twisted metal, jagged pieces of shattered window glass and Roddy's gold watch. Except for the rustle of wind blowing snow across the street and the hissing of steam rising from the cars, there was no sound at all.

Tom Raupp lost consciousness for a moment. When he awoke, pieces of the Oldsmobile's windshield lay in the backseat. Shaken and battered, Tom and his parents scrambled to safety and shouted for help.(8)

Bob Lyndall dashed from his house on Aspen in such haste that he later could not recall if he grabbed a jacket. Jim McGowan ran down his driveway and saw the wrecked cars and clouds of steam lazily lifting into the air. Alex Grether put down the telephone, walked to the bedroom window and saw the flashing red light of a police car. "There's a wreck on Maple," he told Schaeffer. "Meet me over there." (9)

The flashing red lights were atop Duncan's patrol car. The black Galaxie's frame was shattered and resembled a V with the front and back ends pointed skyward. The driver's door was open and it quickly became apparent that Drothler was dead. As Duncan carefully walked about the Galaxie, Grether and Schaeffer tagged along, making their way toward the battered Skylark. They saw Bruce Berridge lying unconscious on his back, half in the street and the

89

other half on the curb. He was so far away that Schaeffer wondered whether he had been in either car.

They peered inside the darkened Skylark. The only movement and sound was from Mike Adair, lying face down in the front seat. He was thrashing and moaning.

"Hold him," Duncan calmly ordered Grether. "Don't let him move."

Grether leaned over the twisted remnants of the steering wheel and pressed down on Adair. He couldn't see Mike's face, but he was sure the boy's ribs were broken. "Don't move," Schaeffer told the unconscious Adair. Then quickly realizing they needed help, Schaeffer ran to the neighbor's house where his father, the physician, was playing bridge.

Duncan put in a call for ambulances to transport the kids to William Beaumont, the nearest hospital. Throughout the small police force, Duncan was known for his unruffled behavior and tonight wasn't any different. "I've got an accident here and I need some help," Duncan coolly said over the radio to Patrolman Harold Jones. Duncan's voice sounded so composed that Jones assumed it was a routine accident. When he saw the mangled cars, Jones was stunned.

"We got a bunch of kids in this car," Duncan said. Jones walked to the Skylark where he saw a motionless girl. Her blonde hair gave him a start. She looked exactly like his 14-year-old daughter Kathy. (10)

Dr. Schaeffer was sifting through the rubble of the Skylark. He had seen plenty of catastrophes. As a flight surgeon during World War II, he had patched together American pilots who had been shredded by bullets. He checked the back seat and gently grasped a girl. He pushed down on her chest and listened for a heart beat. He exhaled in despair. He pumped down on a second girl's chest. Then he examined the Skylark's driver lying unconscious on the street. He was barely breathing and not making any sound.

John Schaefer was startled. He recognized the boy on the pavement. "That's Roddy Henderson," he told Grether. Grether realized he was the same swimmer he watched earlier that day.

90

A handful of cars were crawling to a stop. In Tom Lawton's car, somebody mentioned the burgundy car looked like Roddy's Skylark. Lawton wondered where he could find a pay phone to call Corey Van Fleet. John Matthews, a Seaholm swimmer, was on a double date when he saw a flood of flashing lights and pinkish-red flares in his path. Matthews saw Roddy's Skylark resting in front of a large oak tree. The Skylark was so mangled that Matthews thought it looked half the size of a normal car. Sandy Clemens and her date rolled past the two cars, with her date hoping Sandy would not recognize Roddy's car. A growing crowd stood on the sidewalks just behind the snow banks, the blend of white-street lights and red police lights creating an eerie glow.

Another Seaholm swimmer, Graham Bullock, was no more than half-an-hour behind Drothler on Maple, driving toward uptown Birmingham. He and his date found themselves in a traffic jam and he slowed his car to a crawl. They saw the black Ford and burgundy Skylark. Noticing a friend standing on the curb, Bullock rolled down his window. "It's Roddy and Peachie," the friend said.

Others knew something was wrong, but they did not know exactly what. Nancy Ackerly joined her parents and brother in the front yard and gazed down Maple, but all they could see and hear was the unceasing wail of ambulances and police cars dashing down the street. Bill Keough, a junior and Roddy's close friend, was parked in a car with a date. Somebody, they realized, must have been in a terrible accident.

The paramedics lifted Peachie, Sandy and Drothler into the ambulances. They gently picked Roddy and Bruce from the pavement while scooping up Mike from the front seat almost as if they were yanking out a sack of potatoes. The ambulances raced to Beaumont. Roddy's faint pulse stopped a few minutes after the ambulance reached the hospital. From the moment of the impact, he had been unconscious. It was an absolute certainty that Roddy, Peachie, Sandy and Drothler never knew what happened. (11)

A few blocks away, Susie Martin waited for Mike and his friends to get to her house, but by 11 p.m., she assumed they had changed their plans. She went to bed. A couple of hours later, the phone rang. Susie's mother answered it and learned about the crash. She decided to let her daughter sleep. (12)

Betty and Robin Adair were laughing and joking over cards when the telephone rang. Betty's brother Fritz Adams answered and in a moment returned. "Mike's been hurt, we've got to get down to Beaumont," Fritz announced. Dick Straight, one of the salesmen at the party, volunteered to drive, and Dr. Adair, Betty, Fritz and another physician joined him. Straight drove his Chevrolet to Maple. Far down Maple near the waterfalls, he saw a blaze of flashing red lights. Rather than navigate his way through those police cars, he chose a longer route to Beaumont. (13)

Ed and Helen Henderson were already in the first-floor waiting room. The Grace Kelly film was nearly over when Beaumont Hospital called. In a flash, Helen "nearly flew out of her chair," and dashed to the coat closet. Nancy walked upstairs to her room and sat on the edge of her bed. She cried for a moment. Then she prayed. Roddy would be OK, she assured herself. The roads weren't icy; the accident could not have been that terrible. At worst, Roddy would have a few broken bones. (14)

Helen approached Betty Adair in the waiting room. "Roddy and Mike have been killed," Helen said quietly. Betty felt numb, but maintained her steely composure. She did not want to cry. "Not that good kid," she told herself over and over, thinking of Mike. "He's such a good kid." (15)

Dr. Adair, who knew his way around Beaumont, made his way to the emergency room with his friends tagging along. Straight peered inside and spotted Mike. Despite what Helen Henderson told Betty Adair, Mike was very much alive. Straight swallowed three times and gently placed his hand on Robin's shoulder. "That's Mike on the table." (16)

Dr. Adair did not recognize his son. That's not Mike, he said. Windshield glass from the Skylark had shredded Mike's face and he had a large hole on his forehead. Doctors removed his shoes, cut away his bloodstained corduroys and peeled off his maroon Seaholm letter jacket. Dr. Adair quickly adopted the role of the objective physician rather than the horrified parent. In a calm, business-like fashion he peppered the attending physicians with questions. A few feet away, an unconscious Bruce Berridge lay on a cot, hidden from view by a curtain. Bruce had suffered a concussion, compression fracture in his lower back, broken arm and leg and shattered teeth. Straight sensed he did not belong and quietly left for the adjacent waiting room. There, a large crowd of friends and relatives were gathering: Ken and Rita Berridge; Jack and Betty Barnum; a minister from a nearby Presbyterian church, and Roddy's friend John Allman. A pessimistic Dr. Adair emerged from the emergency room and gently warned Betty: Mike would not live through the night. Betty refused to believe him. They waited in lounge chairs, the evening's quiet punctured by piercing screams from the unconscious Bruce Berridge. (17)

Corey Van Fleet arrived at Beaumont. Tom Lawton had found a pay phone and telephoned the coach at his home. "There's been a bad accident. Rod's hurt bad. They've taken everybody to Beaumont." Now Van Fleet and his wife Mary were in the waiting room, where they saw the Hendersons.

"We've lost Rod," Helen said.

She asked Van Fleet for a favor. "We need somebody to go in and identify all the people and they won't let us in." Without removing his heavy winter jacket, Van Fleet poked his head inside the emergency room. Roddy and Drothler were lying on separate tables. A short distance away, he saw the team of physicians working on a young boy whose head had swollen into a large circle. He assumed the boy was Mike Adair. (18)

When Van Fleet returned to the waiting room, Mary was shocked by his appearance. She had always regarded her husband as one of the most unruffled people she ever met–"Mr. Calm" in any crisis, she liked to say. Instead, her husband was shaking, fighting back tears. She had never seen him lose it like that.(19) He was still struggling to compose himself when Free Press sports writer Hal Schram reached him by telephone. "His future was so bright," Van Fleet told Schram.

"Who knows how far he might have gone; how good he might have been? And now, just like that, it's all over. How can anything be important?" (20)

One floor above in an operating room, a team of physicians worked to save Mike's life. Bob Pool, a 34-year-old plastic surgeon, had been on call at his Birmingham home that night when a nurse telephoned. "We've got a terrible accident," she said. "We have a boy with his face smashed in." Ten minutes later, Pool arrived at the hospital where he joined Hans Beyer, an anesthesiologist; Kenneth Wood, a thoracic surgeon, and Phil Huber, a neurosurgeon. Mike had a fractured collarbone, eight broken ribs, fractured sternum, a punctured right lung, a depressed skull fracture that extended from mid-face through the forehead, and a partial tear in his aorta.

Mike had lost so much blood that his blood pressure had plunged to an alarming rate of 50 and his skin was a deep blue. Wood re-inflated Mike's punctured lung. Beyer skillfully inserted a tube into Mike's trachea, which allowed him to breathe. Next, Beyer attached three intravenous tubes to fill Mike's arteries with blood. To their alarm, Mike's blood pressure stubbornly refused to rise. Each physician took a turn at pressing down on the bags of blood to keep the blood flowing through the tubes.

"Keep pumping, keep pumping," Beyer ordered.

Beyer guessed that Mike had ruptured his spleen and damaged his liver, which was causing massive internal bleeding. What none of the doctors could have possibly known that night was blood seeped through Mike's aorta. Finally after an hour of pumping and prodding, Beyer reported that Mike's blood pressure was starting to stabilize.

Pool and Huber went to work on Mike's shattered face, which had ballooned up to twice its normal size, a clear sign that blood and air had inflated Mike's head. Pool grasped Mike's nose, which had been jammed inside his face, and tugged it back to its normal position. Pool and Huber cleaned away the crushed bones between Mike's eyes and nasal passages. Then they wired his frontal facial bones together and closed him back up. None of them were sure Mike would live through the night. (21)

In her customary way, Betty Adair was taking charge. She had five other kids to worry about and she had no idea when she and Robin would get home from Beaumont. Gwen Straight offered to spend the night at the Adair home. Betty asked if she could help Jim and David deliver the Free Press in the morning. Next, Betty telephoned her daughter Sue, a senior at DePauw University in Indiana. Betty called home where Ellen and her boyfriend were still watching TV. Go get Nancy from her friend's house, Betty ordered. (22)

When Ellen arrived, Nancy was puzzled because her mother wasn't driving. Nancy edged into the back seat and noticed her sister "being sort of strange."

Finally Ellen said, "Roddy and Mike were in a car accident and Roddy is dead."

Nancy was sure her sister was telling a macabre joke. "Nancy, it's true," Ellen shouted in frustration, "It was Mike." For the rest of the drive, nobody exchanged a word. Nancy stared quietly at the back of Ellen's head. She felt very, very lost.

Others were finding out as well. Mike's cousin Bob Adams returned to his house shortly after 11 p.m., expecting to find Robin and Betty Adair playing bridge and the usual cheery "Hi honey, how did you make out?" greeting from his mother. Instead, Adams noticed a deep gloom, as people quietly sipped their drinks. Finally he asked, "What happened?"

"Cousin Mike was in a terrible accident," his mother answered.

"Is he dead?" Adams asked.

"No. But several are," his mother said. She didn't know their names.(23)

Carla Jolly, a Seaholm sophomore who lived next to Peachie on Yarmouth, had just returned from dinner with her parents when the phone rang. "Can you tell if Peachie is at home?" a friend asked. Carla peered out the window and saw a blaze of lights on at the Barnum house. "There's been an accident," her friend explained. He had heard it on the radio. "It's a blonde girl and they say she's from

Barnum." Carla was worried. Could it have been Peachie? It would have been easy, she thought, for a radio announcer to confuse her last name with Barnum Junior High. (24)

Sandy Clemens had reached her house in Troy, a few miles north of the crash. She went to her mother's bedroom and in a daze said she thought she knew the people in the crash. They turned on the bedroom television to watch the news.

The police slowly cleared Maple Road of debris. Two tow trucks hauled the Skylark and black Ford to nearby gas stations. Shortly before midnight, Betsy Brenton and her friend left the Birmingham Theater and drove past the twisted Skylark, now resting at a nearby Shell station. "I hope we don't know anybody in that car," Betsy said. (25)

Dr. Schaeffer was back at his house on Aspen. He poured himself a hefty glass of Scotch and sat down without speaking. His son John was stunned at his father's appearance. He knew his father had dealt professionally with hideous war wounds. That had been his job. But on this night, Dr. Schaeffer seemed more visibly shaken than at any other time in his life. Years later, John could not forget the sight of his shocked father quietly sipping his drink. (26)

Corey Van Fleet was also struggling to make sense of what had happened. They had all been good kids, he thought. They came from earnest, hard-working families who followed the rules of the American Dream. This wasn't the way that dream was supposed to end. The gruesome scene in the emergency room, he would say years later, was the most powerful "testimony to don't drive drunk" he could imagine.

SEVEN

"I don't think I can swim Friday."

Nancy Henderson was upstairs in her bedroom when she heard a car in the driveway. Her parents walked in through the back door accompanied by a woman Nancy had never seen before. Helen slowly approached her daughter and said, "Roddy's dead." Roddy was not to blame, Helen explained. A driver who had been drinking hit the Skylark, killing Roddy, Peachie and Sandy. Bruce and Mike were at Beaumont. Then Helen introduced the woman: She was Corey Van Fleet's wife.(1)

Nancy slowly walked upstairs and sat on the edge of her bed. Her mother and father joined her. Nancy asked a few questions, and they did their best to answer. Nancy tried to get some sleep, but kept waking up as she veered from one nightmare to another.

The Barnums and Christmans had also returned to their homes, accompanied by Corey Van Fleet. The Christmans walked across the triangle to the Barnum house, which seemed a magnet for neighbors. (2)

Nobody seemed to know what to tell 10-year-old Krisa, who was still across the street with Suzanne Witbeck. All Krisa knew was that Peachie had been in an auto accident. Assuming Peachie had broken a leg or arm, Krisa asked Suzanne, "Do you think she'll let me sign her cast?" She thought it was great fun to be sleeping at Suzanne's, although Krisa thought it odd that Suzanne seemed to be sniffling and crying. What's wrong, Krisa kept asking? Just a bad cold, Suzanne replied. (3)

The Adair house was dark when Gwen Straight, her parents' friend, arrived. Assuming the kids were sleeping, she curled up on a couch in the living room. But upstairs, Nancy Adair couldn't rest. Shortly after two in the morning, she opened the diary she faithfully kept and began scribbling. "Oh God, this was the worst day. Roddy dead! Sandy Christman–dead, and Peaches Barnum dead. Mike and Bruce in terribly critical condition. Oh God, it was so awful." (4)

Jim Henderson was still trying to enjoy himself at his fraternity party at Michigan State when a friend called him to the pay phone. "Jim, this is dad. I've got bad news for you. Roddy's been killed in an auto accident." He marveled at his father's seeming calmness. He seemed so composed that Jim replied, "No, that can't be." But Jim's analytical mind quickly turned to the practical. How could he get home?

"I'll probably come home in the morning," he told his father. "I'll get one of the guys to bring me home."

Jim returned to the lobby where the fraternity mother immediately asked what was wrong. He broke down sobbing. The fraternity mother escorted him to her apartment and throughout the night, his buddies surrounded him. He thought of the previous week when his parents told him he could not have the Skylark. Had they said yes, Roddy would still be alive. A few fraternity brothers volunteered to drive him back to Birmingham that night. When he woke up the next morning, his first thought was that somehow Roddy was still alive. (5)

Not far away on the Michigan State campus, a fraternity brother told Bruce's older brother Jim to call home. Ken Berridge explained that Bruce was in the hospital. He might not live. A couple of friends drove Jim back to Birmingham.

Jacquey Barnum had returned from her date and was talking with a few sorority sisters when the housemother appeared in the room. Her father was on the downstairs phone. She was stunned, but immediately wondered how they would break the news to Patty. Jacquey remembered Patty once suffering an anxiety attack and calming down only after breathing into a brown paper bag. So Jacquey hatched a plan: She would get a ride to Patty's dormitory. Calculating exactly how long the ride would take, she instructed her father to wait and telephone just as she entered her sister's room. Unfortunately, Jack telephoned Patty just a minute or two before Jacquey got there. When Jacquey brought her sister back to her sorority house, Patty had trouble breathing. Jacquey handed her a paper bag and ordered her to breathe into it.

A car arrived from Birmingham, driven by one of the Barnums' neighbors. Jacquey and Patty huddled in the back seat for a return trip that seemed to take forever. When they arrived home in Birmingham well after three in the morning, it seemed as if every light in the house had been flicked on. It quickly became obvious that Jack and Betty were so distraught, they could not bear to deal with arranging their daughter's funeral. The job fell to the mature and focused Jacquey. But for this, she was unprepared: She had never even been to a funeral in her life. (6)

All over Birmingham that Sunday morning, people were starting to learn of the accident. The Detroit Free Press carried a brief six-paragraph story on its front page with just the vaguest of details: Four teenagers, the Free Press reported, had been killed in an accident on West Maple. The newspaper identified two of the dead as Roger Henderson and Sandra Christman, but said that "authorities pending notification of their families temporarily withheld names of two of the fatally injured teen-agers." With so little time to produce a story, the Free Press mistakenly reported that Mike Drothler was a teenager too. The sixth paragraph listed Adair and Berridge in critical condition at Beaumont Hospital. It had been a particularly grim weekend in Michigan. Twenty-two people were killed in auto accidents, including eight kids in the Detroit area. The Detroit News did not run a story on the accident, although the paper published an eight-paragraph article about the end of Seaholm's winning streak.

Donna Bell was sleeping at 7 a.m. when she heard her mother call. For a moment, Donna thought she was dreaming. "There's something on the news about a serious car accident in Birmingham and some students were killed," her mother was saying. Ted Blakeslee had just awoken when his mother told him, "Rod's been killed in an accident." He telephoned Tom Lawton for more details. Then he called Chuck Geggie, who at first refused to believe him. "Why are you playing this joke on me?" Geggie demanded.(7)

When Nancy Adair awoke, the aroma of fried bacon filled the house, a sign that her ever-efficient mother was taking care of the rest of her family. Nancy cautiously asked about her brother. "Mike is very serious," Betty replied. Then she went back to her work. (8)

At 8 in the morning, Bill Keough knocked on the front door of his date's house. "Those ambulances we heard," Keough explained, had been for Peachie, Roddy and Sandy. Dave Zimmer, swimming at the U.S. Naval Academy in Annapolis, Maryland, was called to the coach's office. "I have some bad news about someone you used to swim with," the coach said. Bill Saefkow went to 8:30 a.m. service at the First Presbyterian Church on Maple and then stopped by the church office to see his friend Lee Harris, a Seaholm swimmer and the minister's son. Harris told him of the accident. Steve Matthews made his way to the corner of Maple and Lake Park, where debris from the cars still littered the cement pavement. He saw a man's gold and silver Caravelle watch and assumed it was Roddy's. He plucked it from the street and took it home. Somebody should give it to Helen, he thought.(9)

Nancy Henderson awoke to the ring of the doorbell. Who could that be at this hour, she wondered? They were friends of her parents and it was just the beginning of what seemed an endless parade of people stopping by or telephoning. Many brought food, but Nancy did not feel like eating. For the rest of the day, Nancy wandered back and forth from the living room to see friends, or to her bedroom to be alone.

A couple of blocks away, Suzanne Witbeck was walking Krisa down her driveway where she was surprised to see Jack Barnum. "Peachie has gone to heaven," Jack said. Krisa and Suzanne then joined Jacquey, Patty, Donna Christman, and Linda Christman in Peachie's bedroom. Everything seemed so normal, just as Peachie left it. (10)

Donna Bell drove past Roddy's house on Westwood and saw a handful of press cars parked outside. Why couldn't they just leave the family alone, she angrily thought? She continued to Maple and turned left until she reached the bend west of the waterfall. Then she drove uptown where the Skylark and black Galaxie were resting on snow-covered lots at nearby gas stations. She stood there quietly for a few minutes and stared at Roddy's mangled Skylark. Police had roped off the area around the Skylark and an officer stood vigil, urging passing cars not to stop and look. Twice he replaced the rope and tightened it. A young blonde girl looked at the Skylark and ran away in tears. Others gathered at the black Galaxie. One of them was Mike Drothler's father, Fred. He and his wife Dottie had just flown in from New York and now he poked through the twisted debris looking for something, anything, to salvage. "This was my son's car," Fred said to nobody in particular. (11) To his close friends, Fred Drothler seemed inconsolable. "Why couldn't it have been me?" he asked one friend. "Why couldn't they take me instead of Mike?" (12)

On Monday morning, the juniors slowly filed into Room B 104 for their English class. Instead of the usual jostling and laughter, the kids were hushed. To one student, it was a stark reminder of the absolute silence that gripped Seaholm a year earlier when school officials announced the assassination of President John F. Kennedy. They slowly walked to their desks and sat down until just two chairs were empty. One was Roddy's, the other Peachie's. The teacher entered and stood silently for a moment. It was apparent she had been crying. Then she vanished into the hall. (13)

Donna Richardson was afraid to walk into homeroom class where she knew Peachie's empty desk awaited. The homeroom teacher went through the motions of having the class recite the Pledge of Allegiance, but Richardson had difficulty saying the words. (14)

The intercom crackled to the voice of J. Howard Clayton, the assistant principal, who officially announced the deaths of the kids. There would be a viewing of Roddy and Peachie that night in the Hamilton Funeral Home on Maple, Clayton said. Memorial services were scheduled Tuesday for Roddy at the First Methodist Church and Peachie at Christ Church Cranbrook in Bloomfield Hills. Because space was tight, Clayton said only a select few students could attend. Roddy would be buried at the nearby Greenwood Cemetery, Peachie would be placed in a crypt at White Chapel, a few miles away

101

in adjacent Troy. The funerals, Clayton said, would be limited to the immediate families. He did not say anything about burial plans for Sandy, but within hours that day her family held a private ceremony at White Chapel and had her cremated. Clayton finished by canceling the student congress elections and the assembly scheduled for that day. The topic? The dangers of teenage driving. (15)

The Free Press dispatched reporter Walter Rugaber to the school. He found knots of dazed students huddled in the halls and engaged in whispered conversations. Ellen Adair was in her regular gym class when somebody attempted a joke. Ellen laughed, and then quickly noticed friends seemed angry with her. The disbelief was palpable, the silence noticeable. One student thought it "was like watching the whole world blow up in front of you. You saw it, but you really didn't believe it."(16) The band, scheduled to drum up enthusiasm for the elections, was nowhere to be found and only an occasional kid checked campaign posters adorning the walls. To Nancy Yaryan, everything seemed to be in slow motion. "I still don't believe it," Buzz Downey, a Seaholm swimmer, told the Free Press' Rugaber. Suzanne Witbeck explained that she, Peachie and Sandy were like sisters: "I feel like they kind of left me out, like they left without me," she said. (17)

There was no organized counseling by the school. Teachers were left on their own, and some were sympathetic. Ted Blakeslee had sketched a rough draft for an English term paper, but was so preoccupied Sunday he didn't finish. "I can't do this," he told the teacher. "Just give me the grade for the rough copy."(18) Other instructors seemed oblivious to the point of being callous. When Chuck Geggie explained that he had not finished a class assignment, the teacher snapped, "So what?"(19) In Roddy's U.S. history class with its conspicuous empty desk, the teacher said, "Roddy wouldn't have wanted us to mourn. He'd want us to get on with our lives." The kids, who wanted to talk about their friends, thought it was cold and unfeeling. (20)

The public address system crackled again: A bomb scare. The kids, listless one moment, now rushed to evacuate the building. Minutes later, they returned to their classes. It was just the usual crank call. (21)

Van Fleet's office was bombarded with telegrams and phone calls. "Sincere regrets to the entire student body at Seaholm for the untimely tragedy of this past weekend," said one from the co-captains of the Battle Creek Central swimming team. "We also would like to express our hope that Mike Adair and Bob (sic) Berridge have a fast recovery." The Cereal Bowl Relays Committee in Battle Creek sent a telegram saying that Roddy "will be remembered by Battle Creek swimming fans for his fine sportsmanship qualities and wonderful performances in the Cereal Bowl Relays. May you, his parents, team, and classmates find consolation in that Rod Henderson probably has made a greater contribution to the world in a few short years than most people make in a life that has spanned several decades." (22)

At Van Fleet's urging, Blakeslee and Lawton spoke to a reporter from the Detroit News. The swimmers described Sunday as "one of the longest days we ever had." Van Fleet tried to explain Roddy's quirky personality to the reporter. "He was a serious boy," Van Fleet said. "But outwardly he loved to have everybody think he had the world on a string." At 3:30 p.m., he assembled the 45-man swimming team. "We have not had just a big loss in a swimmer," Van Fleet said. "This was a good kid and a future good citizen." He called off practice and left school. He wanted to see Mike and Bruce at Beaumont. (23)

Doctors were letting a handful of close relatives visit Bruce and Mike. Jim Berridge was warned about how bad his brother looked, but it still was a shock. Bruce's face was swollen and a front tooth was missing. He was in traction with casts wrapped around his broken left leg and fractured left arm. He suffered from a concussion, a ruptured eardrum and a compression fracture of the lumbar spine. He was in a coma, but thrashed about so much that physicians were forced to tie his hands down and attach an IV to his right leg so he wouldn't jolt it free. Jim felt woozy. For a moment,

Jim was sure he would faint. A nurse escorted him to a stretcher in the hall.

When Jim regained his composure, he returned to the bed and grasped Bruce's right hand. Jim spoke a few words, but there was no sign Bruce heard him. Instead, he swayed about the bed and screamed, "Oh God, no." It was apparent to Jim that Bruce was re-living the instant he saw the headlights of the black Galaxie.

Bruce yanked out one of his teeth. He swore at a priest. He grabbed a necktie worn by his uncle. At times, his language was comical. An elderly woman in another room stopped by and sympathetically asked the unconscious Bruce how he felt. "I feel like shit," Bruce snapped. His swearing embarrassed Bruce's parents, particularly Rita. Where did he come up with these words, Rita naively asked? "We know he's not like that," a nurse gently assured Rita.

When Van Fleet arrived at Beaumont, he was curtly informed that only family members could visit Mike and Bruce. Van Fleet shrugged and made his way to the staff entrance at the rear of the hospital, pretended to be a physician and strolled into One West, the hospital's intensive care unit. He saw Betty Adair standing over Mike, who was housed inside an oxygen tent. Mike's head had been shaved and his face was swollen and cut. Four tubes were connected to his body. (24)

Mike chattered away, but he made so little sense that it was clear he was not completely conscious. He rattled off a series of questions: Did Janice Poplack know what had happened? Why had he been in a hospital for two months? What day is it? How did he get in this bed? He asked Van Fleet the final score of a meet that had not taken place. In an apologetic tone, Mike said, "I don't think I can swim Friday." (25)

Betty was methodically organizing visitors to see her son, selecting Mike's sister Ellen and Janice Poplack. On a clear and cold Tuesday afternoon, Janice returned home from school to find Betty waiting near the entrance to the Poplacks' garage.

"I have a son who wants to see you," Betty said in a tone that was more a command than request.

Janice told herself over and over that no matter how bad Mike looked, she was going to assure him he was fine. Yet the sight of Mike jolted her. He mumbled a few words, but his voice sounded raspy. She wanted to kiss him on the cheek, but his face was too puffy and banged up. So she kissed him on the only part of his face that seemed unhurt – his lips.

"I love you," Mike said groggily. (26)

Mike's cousin Bob Adams also visited, and like Janice, he was apprehensive. What if Mike asked about Roddy, Peachie and Sandy? Bob pleaded with his father to stay with him. "I don't want him to ask any questions and have to deal with telling him." His dad promised, but as they entered intensive care, Dr. Adams paused to get an update from the nurses. Bob found himself in the situation he had dreaded, alone with his cousin Mike. He quickly calmed down. It was obvious that Mike was too wobbly to ask any questions about the crash. As he looked at his battered cousin, Bob could only think of one thing: How would he ever explain that on the night of the accident, he was getting the first hand job of his life? (27)

A dreary rain fell on Birmingham the Monday night after the crash. The desolate weather, Eddie Watkins thought, was fitting. A huge crowd filed into the Hamilton Funeral Home on Maple to see Roddy and Peachie. Sue Melcher's father pleaded with her not to go, warning that the evening would be too agonizing. When she insisted, he advised her, "Look at the back of the casket. Don't look at her. Because you don't want to remember her that way." (28)

When Jim Henderson saw his brother's open casket, he told his parents, "I just don't think it looks like him." They closed the casket and placed Roddy's photograph on top. In the very next parlor, Peachie's casket remained open at Jack Barnum's insistence, even though Jacquey pleaded to close it. Peachie wore a blue and white striped dress that her parents had just bought for her to wear at a dance. At the last moment, Kris Barnum thought of Peachie's gooey,

105

which she had clutched every night as she slept. The family slipped the gooey inside the casket. Peachie's wavy hair seemed even more curly than usual, prompting a girlfriend to say, "She would be so upset if she saw this." Sandy Clemens leaned over and kissed Peachie on the cheek. Sue Melcher shunned her father's advice and peeked at Peachie. "That wasn't Peachie," she told a friend. She vowed never to look at another casket again.

More than 500 people signed the condolence book. There was Josie Campbell, who had gone camping with Peachie. And Donna Richardson, who went to Peachie's famous slumber parties. Carla Jolly, whose parents had driven to Michigan State the Saturday before to fetch Patty and Jacquey. John Allman, who scarred Roddy's nose with a mudball. Ellen Tower, one of Roddy's many girlfriends. Tudy Banes, whose nickname prompted Peachie to scribble a fanciful rhyme in her yearbook. Nancy Yaryan, who served as the master of ceremonies the night Peachie played one of the bathing beauties at the Derby talent show. Corey Van Fleet and his wife Mary. Members of a rival high school swimming team. Ken and Rita Berridge, fresh from the hospital where they had been holding vigil over Bruce. Ted Blakeslee, who barely edged out a flu-weakened Roddy in the butterfly on the last day of Roddy's life, was there. So were Betsy Brenton, who nearly joined the five kids that night, and Nancy Ackerly, who heard the sound of the crash from her house. As she looked about, Helen Henderson did not even recognize half the people. Eddie Watkins, stunned at the vast crowd, kept thinking. "It's not happening." Roddy lived such a charmed life, Watkins thought. He loved every moment of his short life. Nobody quite knew what to say. When he saw Ed and Helen Henderson, Watkins started to weep.(29)

The next day, school officials first balked when Ellen Adair asked to attend Roddy's memorial service. "But I'm Mike's sister," she protested and they relented. Bill Keough, one of Roddy's buddies, sought out Van Fleet to see if his name was included. "Bill, there is no list," Van Fleet told him. "Just whoever wants to go, can go." Throughout the service, Keough stared at the wooden casket and thought, "Well, I'll see you later Roddy."(30) The drive from the church to the cemetery seemed to take forever. The ground was covered with snow except for a brown blot where workers hollowed out a fresh hole. Nancy Henderson kept wondering how could they have dug in the frozen ground.

Anne Le Fevre's parents drove her from Chicago to Detroit for the services. Everything seemed foggy to her. She had been so homesick after leaving Birmingham. She had missed Roddy so much. Now this. She wanted to see Ed and Helen after the funeral, and one afternoon walked from a friend's house near Seaholm to Westwood Drive and the familiar Henderson home. A block away she stopped. She couldn't go into the house.

There also was a service for Mike Drothler at a funeral home in nearby Royal Oak. Robin and Betty Adair unobtrusively entered the chapel, signed a book and sat in back. When the service ended, they left, not knowing what to say to the Drothlers.(31) But Fred and Dottie Drothler felt obliged to say something to the other families, to do something. A couple days later, Jacquey Barnum answered a knock at the door, and, to her astonishment, it was Fred and Dottie Drothler. They wanted to apologize. So for a few minutes, the four parents stood in the front hall and talked about their kids. Fred and Dottie visited the Christmans and Hendersons. Everyone seemed sympathetic. They did not blame Drothler's parents. Then the Drothlers returned east. They planned to bury their oldest son in Pennsylvania.

Nobody could make sense of what Birmingham Police Chief Ralph Moxley characterized as "the worst catastrophe" in the town's history.(32) Roddy and his friends "were not at fault," editorialized the town newspaper, the *Birmingham Eccentric.* "They were en-route home at a reasonable hour after a sensible evening out." Their only mistake, Moxley said, was "being in the wrong place at the wrong time."(33)

Their close friends were shattered. Sandy Clemens, who had nearly joined Sandy Christman that night, wept so much that her mother sent her to bed and called a doctor. The doctor prescribed a sedative and as a precaution ordered Sandy not to drive a car. When Sandy asked to visit the Barnums a couple of days later, Mrs. Clemens drove her and promised to pick her up in an hour. When she returned, her daughter was still inside the Barnum house. So she walked up the circular driveway, knocked on the door and introduced herself. (34)

In just the past three months, a total of five Birmingham-area teens had been killed in auto accidents. John B. Smith, the Birmingham school superintendent, complained that "we are operating at the rate of better than one high school student being killed a month." The Eccentric provided space for readers to write letters. One woman urged that a traffic light be installed near the curve on Maple. "Maybe a traffic light would cost $7,500," she wrote, "but it would certainly be money well spent if it can save the lives of our citizens." A second woman urged drivers and passengers to use seat belts. If the cars were not equipped with seat belts, she added, then people should install them. One reader suggested that state officials issue 16-and 17-year-olds limited licenses, permitting them to drive only during daylight hours, a concept many states in later years adopted. Another reader, warning that "Woodward and Telegraph have become death traps," demanded that the driving age be increased to 18, speed limits be lowered and violators strictly punished. That prompted a testy reply from another reader who reminded everyone that Drothler caused the accident and yet he was 22 years old. "To read these letters, an uninformed person might think that one of the innocent victims had caused the accident," the reader asserted. "The driver of the car with the teenagers died while traveling the speed limit." Yet another reader pointed out that Birmingham police should have revoked Drothler's license after he smacked his car into a telephone pole in 1961.(35)

Hank Hogan, the associate publisher and editor of the Eccentric, wrote that most of the suggestions simply would not have prevented the accident. These crashes, he wrote, would continue to happen "as long as there are individuals who travel at a high rate of speed . . . in highly populated areas. This is poor judgment and none of these theories take people with poor judgment off the road."(36)

Some resurrected an old suggestion of building a teen center, where kids could dance, listen to music, mingle with friends and not drink beer or wine. Helen Henderson and Betty Barnum embraced the idea. The families asked that instead of sending flowers, friends and relatives donate money to the proposed center.

Mike was thirsty. "A glass of water would help tremendously," he kept telling the nurses in a polite voice. He felt discomfort in his throat and nose. Once every day to keep the nasal tube clear, nurses flushed it with cold water, causing an icy sensation in his stomach. He was aware that at least four tubes were connected to him and one night he impulsively yanked them free. A nearby physician rushed to re-attach them. Because he could not move his head, he could only stare at the ceiling. His eyes were riveted on the tracks that linked the privacy curtains to the ceiling. "Boy, I'm never going to forget this," he thought of those tracks.

Mike felt refreshingly cool. For some reason, he was housed inside a large plastic tent. It was so cool inside that he thought it was an air conditioner. When a nurse removed it, he asked, "Can I have my air conditioner back?" He started calling one orderly Andy the Orderly. He heard Andy ask someone else in the room if Seaholm's swimming meet against Kimball had been canceled. Someone else in the room quickly warned Andy not to say anything about Seaholm or swimming.

Mike was certain–absolutely positive–he saw Dr. Dale Christman standing over him. Everything seemed so surreal. He reminded Dr. Dale that he had caddied for him at Birmingham Country Club. Mike asked about Dr. Dale's golfing buddy, Charles Grenadier. He's here with me, Dr. Dale replied. It was Wednesday night, four days after the accident, and Mike Adair was beginning to recognize people and wonder where he was. The next morning, a physician told him he would be transferred from the intensive care unit to a regular room on the fifth floor. He saw his father. My mouth is dry, Mike said. Dr.

Adair rounded up a few chips of ice and placed them in his son's mouth.

I have to tell you something, Dr. Adair said. There was a terrible auto accident, he explained. Roddy, Peachie and Sandy are dead. Bruce is unconscious in intensive care. Mike nodded. (37)

A technician wheeled him to an elevator that would take him to Room 519. Mike saw Roddy's father. "What's he doing here?" a puzzled Mike asked himself. Then it struck him: Ed was visiting Mike and Bruce. Mike thought, "What do I say to him" about Roddy?

Mike was assigned the bed closest to the door, sharing the room with an elderly man, whom Mike dubbed Woody. Every morning Woody reached into an ashtray for a partially smoked cigarette and lit it. Mike thought the cigarette smell was awful, but there was nobody to complain to. Mike settled into a routine. The room offered a radio and he would listen to WXYZ play the same songs over and over: "Ferry 'Cross the Mersey," by Gerry and the Pacemakers; "Rescue Me," by Fontella Bass; "Red Roses for a Blue Lady," by Vic Dana; "One-Two-Three," by Len Barry, and "It Ain't Me Babe," a Bob Dylan song freshly recorded by the Turtles. Robin provided him with a television set, allowing Mike to watch Cazzie Russell and the University of Michigan basketball team play on Channel 50.

As people explained what happened that night, Mike began to recall murky details. Driving his sister Nancy to a friend's house. A hazy scene at Casa Mia, where he and his friends were sitting at a table rather than in a booth. Somebody tossing pizza crust about. But that was it: No recollection of getting in the Skylark, driving through uptown Birmingham or the oncoming lights of Mike Drothler's car. He hoped he never would remember.

By the end of the month, physicians thought Mike had improved so much that they planned to send him home. But Mike had difficulty lifting his right arm. His sister Sue thought his collarbone seemed to stick out. Sue told her father, and doctors discovered a broken and dislocated clavicle, an injury they originally missed because of the swelling in his upper chest. They would have to surgically repair it by wiring the clavicle back in place. Instead of going home, Mike would stay in 519, listening to the same songs and smelling Woody's cigarette smoke. As he pouted, a girl his age from the next room walked in. She had lost both kidneys and faced the prospect of being on dialysis the rest of her life. But she wanted to know how Mike was doing. She seemed so upbeat. As she cheered him up, Mike grew angry for feeling sorry for himself. One more bit of surgery on his shoulder and he would be home.

He felt strong enough to walk down the hall with Susie Martin and check on Bruce. Mike and Susie chatted away, hoping Bruce would recognize them. Instead, Bruce launched into a tirade of curses. Embarrassed nurses shooed Susie out of the room. She plopped on the hallway floor and listened to the endless shrieking.(38) Nobody knew when it would end. "Bruce is still unconscious and we're really worried about him," Nancy Adair jotted in her diary on January 19. "Please God let Bruce become conscious."

Bruce's head ached. He looked up at a woman standing over him and carefully read the nametag on her hospital uniform.

"Where's Roddy?" he asked. He had been unconscious for eight days.(39)

He had no memory of the past week save for a dim recollection of eating pizza crust. He had no recollection that one friend after another visited him, trying to jar him awake. Rita Berridge implored Mark Morden, one of his best friends, to talk to him and see if he could get through. Mark sat by the bed and looked in astonishment at the maze of tubes flowing into Bruce. He asked Bruce if he knew where he was. There was no response. (40)

But after reading the hospital aide's nametag, Bruce's mind gradually cleared. He did not have much of an appetite nor a desire for water. He could not taste food and the oddest sensation was the inability to smell anything. The pain from his head, his left leg, his mouth and his left arm was intense. Doctors told him he would remain in traction until they could determine how badly he had injured his back. But they promised him that he would live.

111

For the next few weeks he rested in the hospital bed. Then orderlies moved him downstairs where they applied wet plaster and molded a full body cast that stretched from his neck down his left leg. The wet plaster felt heavy and oppressive. "There's no way I'm going to be able to move," he thought. But within a day, the plaster dried and seemed lighter. He regained his sense of determination. "This isn't as bad as I thought," he assured himself. For the next two months, he would be enclosed in the cast, unable to move his back or his left leg. When his fractured left arm healed, he had control over both arms and his neck. The doctors told him he would remain in the hospital for another week. Then he could go home. If everything went well, in nine weeks they would remove the cast. Bruce did not sulk or feel sorry for himself. He was glad to be alive. He was unwavering in his belief that he would completely recover. As he explained to friends, "I am a determined person. If I want to do something, I'm going to do it." (41)

EIGHT

"Life as we knew it ended that night."

The week after the accident, Nancy Adair joined some friends at the Raven, Nancy Henderson came down with the flu, and Krisa Barnum skated on her ice-covered front lawn. Betty Barnum arranged for the maid to stop by and iron the clothes, which she fretted, seemed to pile up. The phone rang constantly, friends sent bouquets of flowers and the postman delivered so many letters that Betty wondered if she would ever answer them all. The Boyles, their close friends across the street, invited Betty and Jack over for dinner, and another friend took Betty to lunch.

As a cold rain transformed lawns and streets into solid ice that Tuesday morning ten days after the accident, Betty thought of her daughters at Michigan State. Jacquey was tough and disciplined. But she worried about Patty. She hand wrote a note to Patty, saying that she and Jack "were thinking of you and hope that you're able to concentrate on your school studies and get back to normal. We're all fine–Daddy went back to the office yesterday and it went pretty well. We're really being kept busy. Hope everything is all right and remember we love you very, very much." She signed the letter, "Mommie, Daddy and Kris." (1)

Everyone seemed to have the same thought: Get back to normal. Bruce and Mike were recovering at Beaumont. Seaholm's swimmers defeated Kimball. Jim Henderson and Jim Berridge returned to Michigan State, while Sue Adair went back to DePauw University. Dr. Adair bought the family a new Sony color television set and Nancy Adair spent the night at her best friend's house.

What none of them realized–or could have realized–was that nothing would ever be the same again. "Life as we knew it," Krisa Barnum would later think, "ended that night."

For Krisa, the biggest difference was the quiet. They had laughed so much before the accident. During Christmas, the house was filled with racket. Now the noise had been transformed into dreary solitude. Jacquey and Patty were at Michigan State and there were no more arguments about who was wearing the other's outfits. Gone were the days when Jack would crack jokes over breakfast with Krisa. There were fewer trips across the triangle to see the Christmans. It was the end of the Cranbrook Yarmouth Cultural Society.

The only sound in the house came from Jack. Just about every night, Krisa heard her father entering Peachie's room, crawling into her bed and crying. It was agony for Krisa because "you could hear him crying all over the place." She couldn't talk about the crash because he wept uncontrollably anytime it was mentioned. The crash became a dirty word. The unspoken rule of the house was never to bring it up. Nobody at the time even considered the idea of therapy. Instead, the Barnums buried the accident. Krisa took it upon herself to make her parents happy by becoming the entertainer, an overwhelming burden for a 10-year-old. She only spoke of Peachie with friends, often to gloomily announce that anybody close to her would die.(2)

She thought her father stopped living. He could not bring himself to buy a plot and bury Peachie, so he left her in a crypt at White Chapel. At times, he blamed himself for Peachie's death. He had worked too hard at IBM and always was at the office instead of raising the kids. He became increasingly moody. Jack had enjoyed martinis before the crash, but now Krisa saw him drinking more, pouring straight vodka into a glass filled with ice. Friends worried that he was becoming an alcoholic like his mother.

Within a few months, he underwent ulcer surgery; physicians removed a chunk of his stomach. His relentless drive evaporated; his single-minded determination to advance at IBM vanished. He passed on a coveted transfer to Germany. Nobody who hoped to ascend to the top levels of IBM would turn down a promotion, and for Jack, it was the beginning of the end of his career. Until the black Galaxie rammed Roddy's Skylark, Jack's life had been charmed. Jack had always played by the rules: He put himself through college, excelled as a Navy pilot and worked slavishly at IBM. Those who knew him predicted he would be a major success after the war. As a young man, he dreamed of living "long enough to have a long, white beard." Now after the accident, he told people he would be dead before age 65. (3)

For Krisa, there was an added burden. Her father was filled with dread that he would lose another child, so he tried to exert greater control over his three daughters. He drove Krisa to school every morning and made certain that Betty picked her up. He ordered Krisa never to get in a friend's car, convinced that she would be killed like Peachie. Because of that prohibition, Krisa rarely shopped or dated and did not attend her school proms. Years later she joked that she "was pretty gross looking," but in fact she was a beautiful teenage girl. One of Krisa's best girlfriends, who prided herself as a clever saleswoman, pleaded in vain with Jack to let Krisa go to the movies.

Like Peachie, Krisa worked her way around Jack's restrictions. She once told Jack that she planned to spend the night at a girl's nearby house. Then she joined three other girls to see Sly and the Family Stone sing in downtown Detroit. "If my dad (only) knew half the things I did . . . ," Krisa said years later. At age 16, Krisa horrified Jack by insisting on a driver's license. Jack relented, consoling himself with the thought that if Krisa drove her own car, she would not be in a car driven by someone he did not trust.

When Krisa developed a passion for riding horses, Jack was terrified she would suffer a fall. He couldn't bring himself to forbid Krisa to ride. But if she did the slightest thing wrong at school or around the house, he would ground her, an indirect way of keeping her off a horse. In fact, Krisa was such a skilled rider, there was little danger. She learned to ride as a young girl growing up in Kentucky. By the time she turned 13, she mucked stalls at the Centaur Stables in nearby Novi. Centaur attracted upper middle class riders who could not quite afford the pricier memberships at the exclusive Bloomfield Open Hunt Club. There was a large indoor ring and three long stables where people boarded their horses. Young people earned a few bucks an hour by taking the horses out of the stalls, grooming and brushing them, and cleaning the saddles and bridles with saddle soap. Krisa took lessons and an impressed trainer asked her to ride one of his own horses. She rode Sabot, a white gelding, and Carmel, a pony. Krisa was coordinated, athletic and in time won ribbons at local shows.

To keep Krisa riding, Betty diverted grocery money without telling Jack. But Krisa hankered for her own horse, an idea she knew Jack abhorred. Buy a horse and Krisa would fall, he feared. Finally one evening after Jack drank a few martinis while playing hearts with Krisa and one of her friends, he agreed. But he extracted a pledge from Krisa that she would earn A's in the sixth grade. Krisa's teacher agreed to help her by assigning special projects to improve her grades. When she achieved perfect scores, Jack paid $800 for a horse. Within a year, the horse died, and Jack refused to buy another. So Krisa turned to Jacquey, who, almost to spite her father, bought her kid sister a new horse.(4)

Krisa pleaded with her father to watch her ride, but he offered one excuse after another. Finally, to Krisa's delight, he agreed. Krisa donned Peachie's old ski jacket and wore her own britches and knee-high boots. But when Jack arrived, he saw an ambulance fetch a girl who had been kicked in the temple by her horse. The trainers borrowed Peachie's jacket from Krisa and carefully wrapped it around the girl's head. A shaken Jack never returned. Krisa assumed that he didn't care about her riding passion. She was wrong. When she brought home ribbons, Jack called friends to say, "Look at what Kris did." Years later, a close friend of Jack's told Krisa that all he ever did was boast about his youngest daughter. She realized he loved her dearly. He just had been terrified that Krisa would get hurt.

At times, Jack seemed oddly detached. A few years later as Krisa and a friend smoked a joint in her upstairs bedroom, Jack shouted from another room, "Hey Krisa, you guys OK?"

"Yeah dad."

"You smoking pot?" he asked facetiously. Yes, Krisa answered.

"OK, good night," Jack said and went to bed. Krisa's friend looked at her in astonishment. Jack never had any idea his daughter was smoking a joint.

Jack's efforts to hold the same sway over Jacquey prompted rebellion. They snapped at each other regularly. Jack objected to the man Jacquey wanted to marry, and only grudgingly consented. She, in turn, thought Jack took Betty for granted and never appreciated her as "the glue that held the family together." Betty put up with Jack's increasingly testy manner and his drinking. Jacquey gave up fun-packed weekends at Michigan State to go home and be with her mother. In her quiet manner, Betty Barnum accepted Peachie's death. Betty once confided to a neighborhood girl that after the crash, somebody kept calling the Barnum house and asking for Peachie. The girl was struck by Betty's composure. But there was one rule Betty never violated: She would not talk about Peachie in front of Jack.

Jack had more success running Patty's life because she did not resist like Jacquey nor outwit her father like Krisa. Jack was particularly worried about Patty and he had good reasons. Patty returned to Michigan State, but schoolwork no longer was a priority. Because she could not discuss Peachie with Jack, she spent her spare time with her own friends talking about her sister. She vowed to somehow make up Peachie's loss to Jack and Betty. Perhaps she could live two lives rather than just one. She found herself consumed by guilt. She asked herself why she was alive and Peachie was dead. Patty was older; she should have been the one killed, not her kid sister. She found it impossible to focus on schoolwork. She went to class, but did not study. She earned such poor marks that Jacquey, ever protective, quietly went to Patty's counselors to ask for advice. Patty thought one reason her grades were slipping was because she had too much free time. She was certain if she filled her time productively, she would discipline herself to study more. So she found a job at a university grill. When Jacquey found out, she told Jack. (5)

Jack was appalled. "Patty, you can't do this," he told her, saying she needed to concentrate on school. Not wanting to defy Jack, Patty quit the job, but resented her sister's interference, sarcastically dubbing her "the Commander"–a nickname that stuck. For a time, the relationship between the two sisters became chilly.(6)

By the middle of her junior year, Patty abruptly dropped out of school and went to work at a nursing home in East Lansing. Jack was deeply disappointed, but he seemed to understand that Patty had changed since Peachie's death. A year later, Patty moved back to her parents' home, landed a job at an employment agency and in no time was directing the office. She began dating an old high school steady, Gary Moorhead. Jack was thrilled; of all the guys who dated his daughters, Gary was his favorite. In many ways, Gary was the son Jack never had. Gary, in turn, revered Jack – a man's man, he would say. They watched NFL football on TV or chattered about business while having a beer in the kitchen. Gary was careful not to mention Peachie in front of Jack. When Gary brought an engagement ring over to the house, he handed it to Patty, grabbed a beer from the refrigerator and asked Jack about football on TV. "Who's playing tonight?"(7)

As his second daughter planned her wedding in 1970, Jack continued to watch out for her. When Patty awoke one morning with a sharp pain in her abdomen, Jack put in the call to Dr. Dale, the one physician he trusted with his daughter. Dr. Dale rushed to the house and concluded that Patty had appendicitis and needed surgery. He personally drove Patty to his hospital where he performed the operation himself. He discovered a ruptured cyst on an ovary, which could have killed her. He removed the cyst and appendix.

Within a couple of weeks after the accident, Nancy Henderson recovered from the flu. She had cried about Roddy, but now, like everyone else, she rushed back to the life she loved so much. There was skiing at Otsego Ski Club, and she was thrilled when a cute Austrian ski instructor said good morning. (8) The following week, she joined friends for Friday night skiing at nearby Pine Knob, whose slopes were illuminated by powerful lights. She was so skilled that she often skied without poles, racing through treacherous areas dotted with pine trees. As she bought her ski ticket that night, a young man flirtatiously looked at her long hair and asked, "Your hair is the prettiest I've ever seen. How long is it?" When she entered the chair lift, an attendant known for his wise cracks told a young ski patrolman, "Hey, here's a cute one for you." The patrolman joined her on the chair for the ride up the hill. "Watch out, don't let him put his arm around you," the attendant joked.(9)

For her 14th birthday in February, friends at school presented her with a cake. That night, Ed and Helen showered her with presents—a transistor radio, zipper duffel bag, purse, necklace and two charms for her charm bracelet. Then Ed and Helen capped off the special weekend with a ski trip to Otsego, where once again the Austrian instructor chatted with her. Her heart pounded harder than usual. That night, her parents took her and her girlfriend into Gaylord and dropped them off for dinner at the Sugar Bowl—the only good restaurant in town—followed by bowling and a movie. A week later, Nancy was off again, this time to visit her cousin in Bay City. The girls went to a church event where they danced to "Eight Days a Week," by the Beatles and "Tell Her No," by the Zombies. Nancy then danced slowly with a 16-year-old boy to "Ferry 'Cross the Mersey" by Gerry and the Pacemakers.(10)

She took part in the school's water ballet show, performing adroitly until her long hair flopped over her face and she couldn't see anything. She joined close friends for an evening at the Raven, helped organize a surprise birthday party for her best friend and in April kissed a guy for the first time. Nancy and her friends went to Cobo Hall in May to see the Beach Boys; Mike Adair was there with Janice Poplack, although Nancy did not see him. (11) On Labor Day weekend she had her first date where the boy drove instead of a parent serving as a chauffeur.

She kept up her diary in meticulous fashion, always making a note of the guys she met. But at first, she rarely mentioned Roddy or the accident. When she saw Sandy Christman's younger sister Linda, Nancy wouldn't mention the crash. But she missed Roddy's infectious smile. Like Krisa Barnum, Nancy could not help notice how quiet the house had become. Roddy's shout of "Where's

119

Nancy?" when he burst through the door every afternoon was gone. She occasionally rode her bike to the nearby cemetery, sat near Roddy's grave and then walked down a small hill to the river below. For some reason, she thought, God had decided Roddy had to die. She kept asking herself: How long would she live? What was it like to die? Where did Roddy go? When she sat for a portrait at age 14, the artist captured her melancholy, painting a lovely young girl with a sad expression gently cradling a cat.

On the day before her 14th birthday, Nancy watched Marianne Faithfull on Shindig perform her hit, "As Tears Go By," with its poignant lyrics by Mick Jagger and Keith Richards. A few months later, Marianne Faithfull released a new album featuring "As Tears Go By" and "Come and Stay With Me." Nancy added it to her collection, storing it next to her other albums on the floor. She would close her bedroom door, lean against the golden ottoman and listen to Marianne Faithfull, Judy Collins, Joni Mitchell and Joan Baez, whose songs conveyed the same sense of gloom she felt. She played them on her guitar. She was sure that life beyond the age of 16 would not be much fun. She poured out her fears in a poem she wrote, titled, "Death,"

"To you he came,
But all the same,
You shouldn't be proud.
Oh no, I hope
You've made him happy,
He'll never be sad.
We'll join him soon,
Just you wait, just you wait."

She re-read her poems. They sounded so angry and despairing. But at what? At first, she blamed cars. For her final exam in ninth-grade speech class at Barnum, she wanted to talk about the danger posed by cars. She carefully wrote the speech on nine pages of lined notebook paper and on a June afternoon in 1966, stood before the class of 30 students. Normally, she disliked speaking in front of people, but this time she felt composed, although a friend thought Nancy's knees were shaking. In a clear, calm voice Nancy spoke of the dangers of "pointless accidents caused by cars," which she called deadly weapons. You may or may not know, she said, but "a year and a half ago, I had two brothers that I was just beginning to treasure as I was growing up. They were a part of our family and naturally a large part of my life. And then in a matter of minutes, I only had one brother all because of that deadly piece of transportation. A big part of my life gone, just like that."

She told the class that she often wished that cars did not exist, but conceded "it's really silly to destroy progress." She said that cars have become bigger and more comfortable, but plaintively wondered why the Detroit automakers could not make them safer. "Why don't people realize that they could make things so much safer and avoid so many accidents by merely being alert and following traffic rules?" she asked. "Why should my brother and two other teenagers with him have been killed just because of a stupid person who had most likely been drinking and should never have been on the road?" She asserted–incorrectly–that more people were killed in one weekend of Michigan auto accidents than Americans every week in Vietnam, asking, "Doesn't that strike you as odd?"

"When you think of war, you think of killing and losing people. When you think of cars, you merely think of a piece of transportation. But it shouldn't be thought of that way because something has to be done about this needless killing. They aren't dying for their country like in war. They aren't dying from old age. They're dying needlessly because people just don't stop to think what they're doing." Her audience loved it, and her teacher awarded her an A. (12)

With her striking looks and long silky brown hair, she was a natural to model. In the spring of 1967, she was a finalist in a modeling contest for Seventeen Magazine at Jacobson's, an upscale department store uptown. She had no shortage of dates, with two or three boys calling every week. But she seemed more interested in finding a brother to replace Roddy than in a romance. One guy in particular reminded her of Roddy. She thought this is the way Roddy would have been had he grown into his 20s. But the boyfriend was perplexed at Nancy's apparent yearning for a friend or brother rather than romantic partner.

When she graduated from Seaholm in 1969, Nancy's parents bought her a car. Rather than being ecstatic, Nancy was reticent. "You know, it's funny about that car," she wrote in her diary. "I'd never admit this to anyone. But I don't really want it. It just goes along with my general dislike of cars. I hate to drive. I hate cars. But they're essential to my life and I'm going to need that thing a lot in the future. I'm really lucky getting it and I'm not saying I'm not really thankful for it, but if a car weren't much more useful, I'd get a horse any day." (13)

For two years after high school, she drove everyday, first working at Centaur Stables, and then at her father's publishing company. At age 20, she was accepted into the early childhood development program at Wayne State University in Detroit and regularly drove to school. On an icy December morning in 1972, she drove down Southfield Road, giving herself plenty of time to make a class. She noticed a police car whizzing by in the opposite direction. The distraction was enough: The car in front of her had slowed down. Nancy slammed on the brakes, but the car skidded on the icy pavement and she plowed into the other car. She banged her knee on the dashboard, causing a bad bruise. She instantly burst into tears. The other driver summoned the police and when the officer examined the two cars, he said, "I like accidents. No two are alike." What a creep, Nancy thought. Nancy carefully turned her car around and drove to her parents' house on Westwood. She cried again. A tow truck hauled the battered car to a garage for repairs. "I'm glad I don't have a car," she wrote the next day. "I hate it."

She moved out of her parents' house to be on her own, settling on a tiny studio apartment on the back of a house in Bloomfield Hills. With its high ceilings and tall windows, the artistic apartment at first appealed to Nancy. But she spent much of her time alone. At night, she read through textbooks from a psychology course. She was depressed and moody. After a few months in the studio, she came to two decisions: She wanted to move back home. And she needed to see a therapist.

Nancy assumed that, unlike herself, everybody else in her family had dealt with Roddy's death and moved on psychologically. Her brother Jim graduated from Michigan State and enlisted in the Marines. Her father displayed his trademark stoic front, remaining composed even during the week after the accident when everyone else was so stunned.

Ed and Helen made a habit of telling the kids how happy they were to still have them and that "Roddy's death was not the total end of our world." Ed bought Jim a new Pontiac even though Jim could not remember asking for a car. In July of 1965, the family flew to Colorado Springs for a vacation, where they went horseback riding, water skiing and took in the breathtaking sights. The following Christmas, Helen and Ed overwhelmed their kids with more presents. The next day the family headed north to Otsego. (14)

Ed had always been an optimist who relished life and outwardly Nancy did not notice any change. Rather than talk about Roddy or see a therapist, Ed went about his normal routine, which meant being preoccupied with work, sports and hobbies. He snow skied in winter and golfed in summer, once scoring a hole-in-one at Bloomfield Hills Country Club. He painted landscapes and listened to his treasured Mozart albums while relaxing in a reclining chair in the den. He kept himself in first-class shape by jogging. He took dance lessons with Helen and joined Nancy and a boyfriend to dance to disco music at a bar. Relying on his World War II experience as a radio operator, he took up ham radio and at night would chatter away with people all over the world. In his determination to stay busy, he joined three different radio associations. The only habit he quit was flying. On a sunny afternoon in 1970 while piloting his Cessna 210 near Flint, he glanced up just in time to see another small plane whiz past. Ed announced that he was through with flying. There would be no more accidents in his life.

But away from Nancy, Ed flashed glimpses of the agony he tried to conceal. Ed cried, but only in front of Helen. Like Jack Barnum, Ed had always known success and never really faced adversity. "You know, maybe I just had things too good," he confided to Jim. He closed two magazines and dropped out of a couple of publishing trade associations, saying he had become disenchanted with them. By the end of the 1960s, the company seemed no larger than the one Ed assumed control of two decades earlier. (15)

Nor did Nancy see any difference in her mother, who appeared to plunge ahead with her life. Helen had always been the family organizer and after the crash, she meticulously sorted through Roddy's record albums and sweaters, and, not wanting them to go to waste, gave most to his friends. She invited Roddy's close friend Dave Nelson to the house. Nelson, who could not bear to even talk about the crash, felt awkward and uncomfortable as he and Helen quietly sorted through Roddy's possessions. She gave him a few shirts and two tickets to see the new film, "The Sound of Music" at the Fisher Theatre in Detroit. (16) Roddy had planned to take Peachie to the film. She gave another friend Roddy's maroon Seaholm letter jacket. She made a point of staying in touch with Roddy's friends; she hosted a wedding shower for Anne Le Fevre in 1968, prompting Nancy to write in her diary, "It brought back memories."

Although Nancy knew her mother was collecting many of Roddy's possessions, she had no idea that Helen had mapped out a detailed plan to keep Roddy's memory alive. Unlike Jack Barnum and others who wanted to push memories aside, Helen could not bear the thought that her gifted son would be forgotten. So she saved. She kept his birth certificate: Roger Leeman Henderson, born at 1:30 in the afternoon, September 29, 1948, at Henry Ford Hospital. She kept his certificate of Baptism from the Central Methodist Church in Detroit on May 27, 1951. She kept scores of photographs–including one of her three kids from Labor Day 1953, with Jim kneeling in front pretending to hike a football, Nancy staring at the ground and an energetic Roddy flashing his signature grin. She kept Roddy's golden watch, the one Steve Matthews rescued from the crash site.

She assembled Roddy's vast pile of swimming awards: A blue ribbon from a swimming meet in Ann Arbor; plaques for the mile swim at Oakland Hills, the 1964 AAU championship in Michigan and the Cereal Bowl Relays a month before his death; a bronze medal as a member of Seaholm's all-American freestyle relay at the 1964 state meet.

Longing for a professional portrait of Roddy, Helen hired an artist to paint her three kids. The artist was forced to rely on a photograph of Roddy, but she captured his lively personality and good looks: His carefully brushed light brown hair in the style of a surfer and his broad smile.

Helen created three thick scrapbooks, each describing a separate stage of Roddy's life. There was "Rod, Book I," a yellow album with the title page: "Roger L. Henderson, 1948-1965." Helen included a black-and-white photograph of Roddy at five months of age. She followed with a photo of five-year-old Roddy riding a pony, a studio shot of eight-year-old Roddy wearing a bow tie, and a color photograph of 13-year-old Roddy atop Brandy, one of his favorite horses. She finished with Roddy's triumphs: A 1962 photograph of the Oakland Hills swimming team with Roddy towering over everyone, and a photo of Roddy standing on the winner's block after an event at the Detroit Yacht Club.

"Rod, Book II" opened to a photo of the Seaholm swimming team shortly after winning the state title in 1964. Next, Helen taped in a Birmingham Eccentric team photograph with the boys politely staring at the camera except Roddy, who could not resist goofing off; he turned his head away as the camera clicked. She pasted in his lifesaving and water safety card from Oakland Hills, a scoring sheet from a 1964 meet and a photograph published in the Royal Oak Tribune of Roddy poised to leap in the water. The publication date was January 1965.

On the inside cover of "Rod Henderson, Book III," she pasted a color photograph of Roddy, Mike Adair, Bruce Berridge and Mark

Morden taken in happier days in the Henderson living room. On the opposite page, Helen attached the large maroon and white letter B from Roddy's Seaholm varsity jacket. Then she followed with scores of newspaper accounts of the crash, including Dick Zemmin's touching sports column from The Eccentric in which he wrote that Roddy "possessed the scarce requirements needed to make a performer stand out among others, the prerequisites to blaze a trail in the field of athletics that only a handful of athletes do possess."(17) There was Roddy's whimsical swimming poem, a sermon offered at one of the memorial services and a photograph of Roddy's oil painting. She treasured the albums, but kept them to herself, waiting for years before she told Nancy of their existence.

Helen also helped conceive an idea to build a teen center, which would serve as the ultimate monument to Roddy. The center would allow kids to mingle, dance, chow down on snacks and have fun without drinking beer. The Hendersons, Christmans and Barnums were all enthusiastic, but they needed at least $50,000 to refurbish an existing building. They asked friends and relatives to contribute money to the center instead of sending flowers to the funerals, and by November had collected $3,500. Then they got a break. A donor who asked to remain anonymous offered $15,000 if the kids and families raised the remaining $35,000 on their own. More than 800 students from Seaholm, Groves and Brother Rice High Schools peddled booster buttons by walking through neighborhoods and sold $3 membership cards to more than one thousand kids. They wrote letters to potential donors, washed cars on weekends and organized a march through uptown to ask merchants to pitch in. (18)

They found an ideal location uptown on Brownell, just off Woodward and Maple – a large building that had a few months earlier housed the Raven and a furniture store. The owner agreed to a lease, paid the first year's taxes of $400 and contributed another $1,000 to the memorial fund. A local architect offered to design the center. He included a 6,500-square foot dance hall that could accommodate 800 kids, a snack bar and Coke parlor, a carpeted TV lounge, pool tables and ping-pong tables. The families selected a director to manage the center.

On a Saturday in January of 1966–one year after the crash– Michigan Governor George Romney and his wife visited the nearly completed center. "This is the kind of activity that built this country," Romney said. As the governor spoke, the Hendersons, Barnums and Christmans stood quietly off to the side. (19)

When the center opened in the spring of 1966, Ed and Helen were among the first to volunteer as chaperones. "It is a credit to the many teens and adults who labored long and lovingly to bring about its fruition," The Eccentric wrote in an editorial.(20) Just about every weekend night during the first three years, the teen center was packed. The area's best bands–Bob Seeger System, Scott Richard Case, Harmon Street Blues and Ourselves–performed some of their own original songs or familiar sounds of the mid-1960s. Sometimes the center sponsored Combo-Clashes, a special treat where more than one band showed up. Nancy was a regular. (21)

But after a couple of years, the center lost its attraction. Kids went back to cruising Woodward or scattering to other dance clubs, like the Hideouts in Southfield or the Silverbell Hideout in Lake Orion. It became increasingly difficult to find the $25,000 to operate the center every year. The name was changed to the Village Pub, and not long after the dance hall and snack bar closed, replaced by a cozy coffeehouse. Helen was deeply disappointed; a connection to Roddy had faded. "Like so many things, kids think they want it and then they don't use it," she said years later. (22)

At times, Helen was so expressionless that Nancy wondered if she ever showed any emotion about Roddy. But late at night after Ed and Nancy had fallen asleep, Helen would head to the first-floor den in the back of the house, just off the living room. She would sit in a reclining chair or at a large desk with the built-in bookshelves behind her and tenderly examine a pile of old letters from close friends and relatives. "Somehow words seem very inadequate at a time like this as we try to express our sympathy," wrote an old friend in San Francisco. From Chicago, Anne Le Fevre wrote that one of her friends "used to kid me about my 'Roddy smile' because she could always tell if I was thinking about him. She said my whole face lit up . . . I have so many wonderful memories that when one comes back, my face cracks into a 'Roddy smile.' "

Then there was the letter from Suzanne, a girl she could not recall meeting. "Please don't take this as just another letter from anyone, but from a person who loved your son dearly and spent over a year of happiness with him," Helen read. "I know the pain and heartache you went through and my heart aches for the fine family he grew up in. And Mr. and Mrs. Henderson, my compliments are for you for your beautiful job of raising a perfect and wonderful guy. I loved him dearly for quite awhile and I know the loneliness you feel, for I feel it also."(23) There was another letter praising Roddy for serving as a swimming coach to the younger kids at Oakland Hills, much as he had coached Nancy. Helen was surprised. Roddy never said anything about coaching. Over and over, she would read the letters. Then she would cry.(24)

Nancy's decision to see a therapist in 1972 was not the first time she had tried counseling. Not long after the accident, her parents sent her to see a therapist, but she stopped after a few sessions because she couldn't think of anything to say. But gradually, she realized something was terribly wrong. As a high school junior, she read Joshua Loth Liebman's 1946 book, "Peace of Mind." Throughout the 1930s and 1940s, Liebman, a rabbi, attracted large radio audiences with his blend of religion and psychotherapy. Nancy scribbled in her diary, "Repressed feelings because of death." Then she copied passages of Liebman's book in her diary: "A number of patients had repressed their real feeling of guilt and as a direct result of that repression, many morbid reactions sooner or later made their appearance. Some people were living a life of rage and anger against the world without knowing why." She wrote that Liebman believed you should "express as much grief as you actually feel." Then she scribbled another paragraph from the book: "When death destroys an important relationship, it is essential that someone be found partially capable of replacing that relationship. I often feel that death is not the enemy of life, but its friend for it is the knowledge that our years are limited which makes them so precious." After she finished copying, Nancy wrote, "I am finding this very thought provoking. This is part of my search – a search for God, purpose, future, happiness, and understanding of myself." (25)

Now, four years later–and just days after her car accident on Southfield Road–she began regular sessions with a therapist. This time she wanted to talk –about Roddy, boys in her life and her passion for writing. Within a few weeks, Nancy felt she had discovered someone she could trust, someone who would listen to her. In her rush to resume her regular life, perhaps she had not grieved about her brother? How much was she supposed to cry about Roddy, she wondered? The therapist urged her to re-read her diary from 1965 and 1966.

The sessions jarred her, sparking memories that she had long suppressed. While dozing in the back seat of her parents' car in January of 1973, Nancy saw the image of another car turning in front of her father's path. She opened her eyes: It had been a nightmare, she realized. Three nights later–exactly eight years after Roddy's death–Nancy dreamt about a horrifying auto crash. A few weeks later, she walked about her darkened house at night. The familiar lights that illuminated the hallway were off. She flipped the switch, but nothing happened. She was certain she was blind. Then she awoke with a start; it was yet another nightmare. She leaned back in her bed and wrote down everything she could recall from the dream. "Something about losing Roddy hit me like it never hit me before," she scribbled. "Finally I felt all the resentment and hurt that I was entitled to."

For the first time, she recognized she was angry about losing Roddy instead of disliking cars. The next day she sat at a table in one of the buildings at Wayne State and cried. When she returned home, she took a long walk near Quarton Lake, not far from where Roddy was buried. She watched the ducks land on the thin ice forming on the river that fed the lake. There were footprints in the freshly fallen snow. She sang aloud. She wondered how her life would be different had Roddy not died.(26)

She began to talk more openly about the accident. She explained to her boyfriend that she often resented him for not being the brother she missed so much. She knew he couldn't be a brother, that he didn't want to be a brother and he had done nothing wrong. It was her problem to work out. She listened to rock music, particularly songs by Melanie, Joni Mitchell, Kiki Dee and Neil Young, and when she heard a song that she identified with, she scribbled the lyrics in a yellow spiral notebook. There was "Wildflower," a hit in the spring of 1973 by the Canadian rock group Skylark – "And when her youthful world was about to fall in." She pored through the poetry of Theodore Roethke, whose life as a teenager was scarred by his father's death in 1923.

She was "getting somewhere," she wrote in her diary. (27) That fall of 1973, she decided to transfer to Oakland University, closer to her home. Before she started classes, she went on a camping trip to Vermont with a friend who was moving there. She drove back to Birmingham by herself. "I'm on my way again and I feel calm and good inside – like I'm finding my way slowly, but surely." (28) Her therapist said she seemed more confident and less anxious.

On a Friday evening in January of 1975, she sat in her room, just across the hall from Roddy's old bedroom and composed a poem that began, "Ten years ago, last night." Writing with a blue pen, she rapidly scribbled lyrics, brief lyrics without punctuation, but lucid and very different from her teenage poetry. The crash, she wrote, "made no sense." She had been so happy that day – "laughing and playing." Then in an instant it all changed. Roddy was gone.

"He will always live
In my heart
Goodbye Roddy
Take care."

It was dark outside. She closed her notebook. She had no intention of ever showing the poem to anyone.

A few months later on July 4, Nancy went by herself to the pool at the Oakland Hills Country Club. While others laughed and splashed, she tanned herself while relaxing in a lounge chair. She thought of those innocent days when she and Roddy swam all day at the club on the Fourth of July and then plopped down on the fairways at night to watch the fireworks. On this day, though, the Fourth of July was unbearable. She left the club in late afternoon and went home to watch TV. Near dusk, as most people in Birmingham watched fireworks or grilled out with their friends, Nancy went to the nearby cemetery where Roddy was buried. She folded her hands, bowed her head and said a silent prayer. Then she returned home and dashed off more lyrics: "Remembering the past too clearly, and its effect on you now."

She earned her degree in elementary education later that year and celebrated by moving to Aspen for a few months where she often snow skied with a group of guys. There was a trip to Europe to visit a girlfriend and a vacation in Mexico. When she returned to Birmingham, she regularly played racquetball. She worked as an editor at Business News and was known as a stickler for accuracy, catching typos and misspellings that others had missed. She met an old boyfriend for drinks and a movie. He told her she had changed for the better. She seemed, in his words, to have a different "air" about her.

In December of 1976, she moved out of the Westwood house and into a first-floor one bedroom apartment on Adams Road, just three blocks from Business News, allowing her to walk to work everyday. She furnished the living room with a new sofa, a rocking chair she bought from Pier One and a maple wood dining room table with four chairs. She lugged her double bed from her parents' house and placed the mattress and box spring directly on the floor. So many high school friends and old boyfriends were home for the Christmas holidays, that she held a house-warming party the night before New Years Eve. Guests brought their own guitars, with one woman showing up with a banjo and a guy bringing a mandolin. Nancy joined in with her own six-string acoustic guitar, playing folk songs as they drank beer and smoked a few joints. The next evening, Nancy celebrated New Years Eve by snow skiing at Pine Knob with her boyfriend and another couple.

After the New Year, she started showing up when her boyfriend's band practiced, and soon the other guys in the group persuaded her to sing. She bought a microphone and tambourine. When she first listened to the recordings, she thought she sounded lousy. Still, she kept at it, concentrating on breathing and practicing with the band every night until 10. In September of 1977, they performed at a wedding reception. Wearing a navy blue flowered peasant skirt and a lacy white blouse, Nancy shook the tambourine and sang. Ed and Helen showed up, and Nancy earned $175 for the evening. She jokingly described it as her "somewhat bizarre singing career," but years later felt a sense of loss because she gave it up. It was too grueling, she thought at the time, to work during the day and practice singing at night.

She had begun the process of understanding why she was so angry. But there was something else: She was nagged by the fear that if she enjoyed life, it would come to an end. Roddy loved life and he died. So would she. "Yesterday marked 12 years since Roddy's death," she dutifully noted in her diary. And yet there was still a hole in her life. Roddy, the person she most looked up to, was gone and no one could replace him.

Bruce Berridge in recovery, 1965.

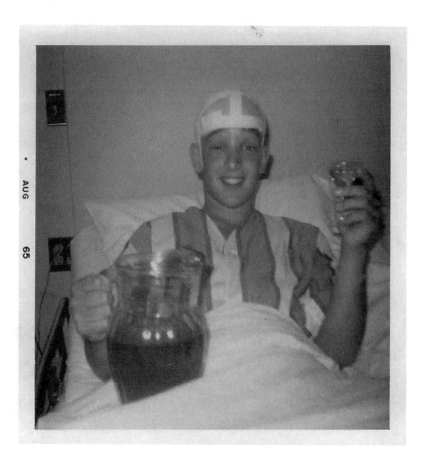

Mike Adair in hospital, 1965

NINE

"I just came to see Roddy"

Mike Adair left Beaumont Hospital the first week of February of 1965. Before the crash, he had weighed 140 pounds, much of it muscle developed by Van Fleet's grueling workouts. Now his weight had plummeted to 110 and his white Levi's slipped to his hips. Mike's face would periodically bleed and to the astonishment of his friends and family, he would calmly remove another fragment of windshield glass from his skin. In the center of his forehead he had a depression about the size of a silver dollar, a vivid reminder of where he slammed into the radio knob. Even though skin had covered the hole, his buddies could see his pulse. He looked so banged up that his father dubbed him Scarface.

Betty and Dr. Adair wanted Mike to get back to a normal schedule and that meant returning to Seaholm. At the end of February, he went back for two hours a day, building to four hours the next week, and all day by the third. He took Janice Poplack to a Seaholm swimming meet. Corey Van Fleet shook his hand and friends waved. When the meet ended, Dr. Adair collected Mike and Janice in the school parking lot. As Mike slid into the car, he felt a stabbing pain in both shoulders. He was in such agony that he forgot to say good night to Janice. When the pain eased an hour later, the ever-efficient Betty advised, "I think you better call Janice and tell her you're all right."

Ten weeks after the accident, Mike filmed the state swimming meet at Michigan State University for Bruce, who was still hospitalized. Van Fleet warned his team that "everybody thinks we're down and out." Chuck Geggie, who won the 400 freestyle, was Seaholm's only individual champion. But as a team, Seaholm prevailed. It wasn't even close. Seaholm qualified 11 individuals and both relays, fielding competitors in every event except the 200 individual medley and 100 breaststroke. By contrast, Battle Creek qualified just seven individuals and one relay team. Seaholm finished with 160 points, far ahead of Central with 126. But the fun, the laughs, the games of jacks were gone. Every time he walked into the Seaholm dressing room, Ted Blakeslee glanced at Roddy's old locker. The Seaholm student newspaper published Roddy's quirky poem about swim meets and Van Fleet's lousy milk shakes. Tom Lawton, not Roddy, set the state record in the 100 freestyle at the conference meet. As good as Lawton was, Van Fleet knew Roddy would have gone faster, perhaps breaking Zackary Zorn's national high school record of 47.8. "Henderson might have been worth 20 points to us," Van Fleet wistfully said before the meet.(1)

The team scattered. Tom Lawton went to the University of Michigan, Chuck Geggie to Michigan State and Ted Blakeslee to Eastern Michigan University, where he earned small-college all-America honors. Gone too was Corey Van Fleet. After the 1965 state meet, a close friend from nearby Oakland University offered him the chance to launch a new athletic program.

At first, Van Fleet wasn't enthused. "Hell, I can be elected mayor of Birmingham. Why would I want to go out there and start over?"

His friend offered Van Fleet a raise. Van Fleet said no. Then he offered the coach a lot on campus to build a house. Van Fleet began to weaken. Next, his friend said he could build any house he wanted–no money down–and the school would arrange a 3-percent loan. And Van Fleet could keep his summer camp program in picturesque Irons near Traverse Bay.

"You've got yourself an athletic director," Van Fleet said. Seaholm never again would win a state swimming championship.

Van Fleet's friends in Michigan swimming placed a plaque honoring Roddy in a corridor opposite the Seaholm swimming pool. Mounted on a wood base, the plaque consisted of a golden swimmer poised to dive in the water. It read: "This plaque stands in fond memory of a superb competitor who lived as an inspiration to all who knew him."

Mike's friends and family showered him with gag gifts, including a coloring book and a bottle of bubble soap. Mike took a deep breath and exhaled as hard as he could, but only a solitary bubble emerged.

136

He knew what that meant: His punctured lung had not healed. In April, his father drove the family to Del Ray Beach in Florida. During the three-day drive, Mike kept himself occupied by carving a bun board from a piece of smooth mahogany. His younger brother Jim was shaken by Mike's appearance–a seemingly oversized Seaholm letter jacket wrapped around a frail body. When Jim cautiously told Mike how skinny he looked, his older brother jokingly replied, "I can still kick the shit out of you." (2)

In July, Mike returned to Beaumont for seven days while surgeons inserted a stainless steel screen into his forehead. Fascinated, Mike asked if he could be awake during the surgery. A doctor shook his head. "We can't put enough local in." They shaved his head, inserted the screen, and wrapped a large bandage around his forehead. Susie Martin visited nearly every day, supplying Mike with Kool-Aid in a champagne glass, snapping photographs as he hoisted the glass.(3)

The bill amounted to $368.40, with $60 to cover the operation–one more addition to Mike's growing medical charges. Beaumont Hospital sent a $1,582.95 bill for his three-week stay in January after the accident. The charges included $486 for 18 days in the hospital; $190 for the operating room; $100 for X-rays; $380.25 for drugs and dressings; $188 for laboratory work, and $65 for oxygen. Birmingham Ambulance Service sent a request for $25 to cover the cost of transporting Mike from the accident scene to Beaumont. Dr. Adair mailed a check for $250 to one of the surgeons, a longtime friend. Within a few days, the surgeon returned it with a handwritten note. "It was rewarding to me to see Mike get through a long and difficult ordeal, and my family is such good friends, I just can't take the check," he wrote. "I hope you will understand that your sincere appreciation is all I want–your confidence in me is full payment." (4)

The Adairs and Berridges reached a financial settlement with Fred and Dottie Drothler. The Adairs and Berridges filed claims in an Oakland County circuit court against an estate that the Drothlers established for their son. In the lawsuit, the attorney for the Adairs and Berridges pointed out that Mike Drothler drove at a high rate of speed, crossed the centerline of Maple Road and "operated the automobile on a public thoroughfare while under the influence of intoxicating beverages." The Drothlers had a $20,000 insurance policy on the black Galaxie and even though Adair's attorney acknowledged "that there is no legal obligation" on the part of the Drothlers "to make any contribution," Fred offered $10,000 of his own money at a time when his annual salary was $19,500.(5) A year after the accident, the families reached an accord: Drothler's father and the insurance company paid $24,825 and the Adairs' and Berridges each took $12,412.(6)

To pay for the settlement, Fred Drothler had to sell a large chunk of his 500 shares of Retail Credit stock, which was then worth $62 a share. But for Fred and Dottie, the emotional anguish was far worse. Mike had been their oldest child and they had spent much of his early years worrying about his heart condition, convinced he would not live long. Then their hopes soared after the successful heart operation. Now this. "It just tore them apart," Bob Drothler would later say. Outwardly, neither Fred nor Dottie showed much emotion about their son's death. They never discussed it with Bob but he could sense "what was going through their minds."(7)

Bruce Berridge's recovery was months behind Mike's. He did not leave Beaumont until March, and when he did, he was wrapped inside his body cast, which he had taken to calling his Elephant Urinal. His parents, Ken and Rita, rented a hospital bed and converted the downstairs den into a bedroom. Propping himself on pillows, Bruce could gaze out the windows on the side and front of the house. Bruce knew he would spend the next nine weeks in the cramped den, but he wasn't discouraged. He had set his mind to making a full recovery. Every day in the den moved him one more step toward that goal.

He had lost 30 pounds and was a sickly 139. The body cast made it impossible for him to bend his back. He could not use a bathroom and relied on bedpans. He could not smell or taste anything. He slept for most of the first few days or passed the time watching "The Man From U.N.C.L.E." and other popular TV shows.

But he was too restless to simply stay in the bed. He set a series of goals for recovery. A goal to walk, a goal to get out of the house, a goal to play sports. He started with baby steps, propping himself up with a metal walker constructed by his father. Like a stiff piece of wood, Bruce climbed out of bed, slipped on loafers, shirt and slacks and tottered about the house. One goal down. He grabbed a golf club and hit a few balls in the backyard. Because he could not use his hips and legs, he relied on his arms to swing the club. It wasn't the way they taught you to hit a golf ball, but it worked so well that Bruce would use the unconventional swing the rest of his life. Another goal achieved. He shot baskets with his buddy Bill Saefkow, which forced him to stand without the walker. He steadied himself, grasped the ball and flipped it toward the basket. He tossed the ball so hard that once he knocked the rim completely off the garage. Another goal attained.(8)

A major goal was simply to stay occupied. Bill Saefkow helped Bruce start his own stamp collection, much like the collection Bill showed him in January just hours before the accident. Bruce began by collecting stamps from all over the world, but switched to those commemorating famous events in American history. To pass the 11th grade, he knew he would have to take his tests at home instead of at school like everyone else. So Bruce asked Bill's sister, a future senior class valedictorian, to tutor him in math, history and English.

As the trees in the front yard turned the first mellow green of spring, Bruce set a new goal: He wanted to go Woodwarding. The Elephant Urinal made it impossible for Bruce to fit into the back seat of an ordinary sedan. So Mike Adair improvised with a buddy's Ford Falcon convertible. No matter how chilly the temperature, they put down the top, hoisted Bruce like a mummy and plopped him into the back seat. Then they drove past friends' houses, honked the horn and pointed to Bruce. If the weather was warm enough, they drove to Ted's or Maverick's, where they could eat the drive-in's signature cheeseburger with its ranch sauce. Another goal realized.

He set a goal of seeing as many friends as possible. Butch Fleming would watch in fascination as Bruce slid a metal coat hangar inside his cast to scratch any part of his body that itched. "When are you going to get out of this bed?" Butch teased. "We've got things to do." Everybody wanted to autograph the Elephant Urinal, with Mike Adair printing his first name in large block letters, and another kid printing, "The Mummy." A regular was his girlfriend, Susie Martin. Because yellow was Bruce's favorite color, Susie made a point of buying yellow outfits for herself. She would bring the latest 45s or fresh cut flowers and tell him jokes. (9) When she dislocated her left knee dancing, she and Bruce rehabilitated together. She would sit on the dining room table, attach a heavy boot to her left leg and lift it. As she held her leg up, Bruce leaned on his metal walker to wobble toward her. Then he would rest in a chair and almost on cue, Susie's Burmese cat Teak would leap on his chest and claw in frustration at the hard cast. (10)

His ultimate goal was to escort Susie to Seaholm's junior prom. A couple of weeks before the prom, physicians removed the body cast and Bruce was struck by how light he felt, almost like a bird. They warned him not to physically push himself, but Bruce shrugged off that advice and started to jog. After spending more than three months in traction and in a body cast, the last thing Bruce wanted to be was cautious. He had too many more goals to achieve.

On the night of the prom, he slipped into a light blue tuxedo jacket and navy blue slacks, and joined Susie, Mike Adair, Janice Poplack and two other friends for photos in front of a cherry tree. Bruce set down the walker and flashed a broad smile. Then they helped Bruce into Mike's car for the short drive to Seaholm. When they arrived, Bruce insisted on getting out of the car without any help. Slowly he made his way up the sidewalk until he reached a wooden bridge that students had built over an imitation riverbed, which was decked with lights. Susie was certain he could not summon the strength to cross the bridge. "We're not doing this," she said.

Yes he would, Bruce replied and gingerly limped over the bridge, joking afterward, "You didn't think I could do it." They entered the gymnasium, which was adorned with murals. One mural was an image of Roddy. Using his walker as a prop, Bruce danced with Susie. (11)

By the fall of 1965, Mike thought he was ready to resume his old life, and that meant swimming. The surgery to repair the hole in his forehead had been successful. He looked like any other kid except that his eyebrows no longer evenly matched. A baffled substitute teacher in English class asked, "Why was one eyebrow lower than the other?" Mike was uncomfortable, but quickly summoned his ever-present sense of humor. "I was in a car accident," he replied. "They probably didn't get my eyebrow on straight." (12)

The first workout was November 1. Mike felt a surge of heartburn just as if he had eaten spicy food. Initially, he ignored it. But when he got home that night, he was troubled enough by the pain to tell his father. Normally Dr. Adair would listen to his kids' everyday medical complaints with a shrug. This time, Dr. Adair peppered Mike with questions. At dinner, Mike ate one mouthful of spaghetti and put down his fork. He had difficulty swallowing because the heartburn had returned.

"Don't go swimming tomorrow," Dr. Adair ordered.(13)

Dr. Adair telephoned a close friend, who was a radiologist at St. Joseph's Hospital in Pontiac. Mike underwent a barium swallow X-ray. The radiologist was stunned: There was a large curve in Mike's esophagus, caused by a ballooning of the aorta, which is the main artery carrying blood from the heart to the rest of the body. He concluded that when Mike struck the Skylark's dashboard and fractured his sternum, the forceful blow weakened his aorta and created a tiny rupture. A ruptured aorta would explain the cause of the heavy bleeding which baffled Doctors Pool and Beyer in the operating room the night of the accident. In the months since, the tiny rupture healed, but the weakened aorta expanded, pressing against Mike's esophagus. The radiologist had only seen one other X-ray like Mike's and the patient had died during surgery. Most people who suffered aneurysms were much older than Mike; an aneurysm killed the great nuclear scientist Albert Einstein.

141

"That kid can end up dead in the pool at any time," the radiologist told Dr. Adair and Betty. (14)

Dr. Adair turned to another longtime friend, Alvin Larson, a surgeon who practiced in nearby Pontiac. Larson told him that Denton Cooley and Michael DeBakey in Houston had pioneered the most advanced procedure to repair an aorta. In 1956, they replaced the damaged area of an aorta with a tube made of Dacron. Larson figured that was the one way to save Mike's life. A call was put in to Cooley. "Mike must have a rupture at the base of the aorta," Cooley said by telephone. Bring Mike to Houston.

Cooley scheduled surgery on Wednesday, November 10, 1965, and the Adairs booked a flight from Detroit. On a frigid Sunday before the flight, Mike delivered his younger brother's newspapers and hoped to join his friends for touch football, shrugging off his father's order to avoid any physical sports. As Mike yanked the newspapers from the car, he slipped on the ice and jammed his shins against the door. Irritated, he kicked the door in anger. His foot hurt so badly, he had trouble walking, forcing him to watch the others play football. That night, Susie Martin and her parents took him to dinner at their private club in Bloomfield.(15)

The next day, Dr. Adair, Betty and Mike flew to Houston where they picked up a rental car, the first time Betty had ever been in an air-conditioned car. They showed Cooley the X-rays, left Mike at the St. Luke's Hospital and checked into a nearby hotel. Technicians conducted an arteriogram to confirm the aneurysm. Now there was nothing for Mike to do except wait. To keep Mike busy, Dr. Adair and Betty drove him to the brand-new Astrodome, the first indoor baseball and football stadium built in the United States. There was no game that night, so the three took a guided tour of the imposing structure, which sports writers had dubbed the Eighth Wonder of the World. The car radio broadcast a report that the entire city of New York had suffered a blackout. Mike's first thought was, "I hope that doesn't happen here tomorrow," fearing the hospital lights would blink out during surgery.

Mike was confident the next morning as nurses fetched him from his room, although he briefly harbored a "maybe this is it" thought. Cooley had developed a surgical procedure based on mass production concepts: One team of surgeons would cut Mike open, a second team would implant the Dacron and a third team would stitch him up. With such techniques, Cooley and his team could perform more than a dozen complicated operations every day. On this particular operation, Cooley conducted the entire procedure. He made the incision, explored Mike's chest and hooked him up to a pump bypass. To Cooley, the aneurysm appeared to be the size of an orange. He removed the damaged section of the aorta and replaced it with a Dacron tube about an inch-and a quarter in diameter. In less then three hours, Cooley was done. From a seat above, Al Larson watched in amazement. He had never seen such speed and efficiency in so complex an operation. "It's everything it's cracked up to be," Larson told Betty. He said that no surgeon in Detroit was "equipped to do this." (16)

When Mike awoke in a recovery room, he felt a stabbing pain in his chest caused by the incisions. He looked around and saw as many as a dozen people who had just been operated on by Cooley's team. Most were much older, but a young boy in the next bed was crying. "Your mother is going to be here," a nurse assured the boy. Everyone else groaned and moaned, almost in a rhythmic beat. As he listened, Mike did something almost nobody ever does in a recovery room: He began to laugh.

Four days later, Cooley invited Mike, Dr. Adair and Betty into his office. The Dacron would last a long time—"pretty permanent" he said years later. But Mike had to exercise some caution. Keep jumping to a minimum and under no condition during the next year should he dive from a diving board. A few months later, Mike joined some friends swimming at a quarry. Impulsively, Mike climbed to the top of a 10-meter diving board and jumped. As he tumbled toward the water, he suddenly recalled Cooley's admonition. "Whoops," Mike thought as he splashed into the quarry. The Dacron held. (17)

Both Mike and Bruce were getting physically stronger by January of 1966. But a crash of which they had no memory was now a permanent companion. The lives they once led, the fun parties at Ellen Tower's house, the gatherings in uptown Birmingham, and the thrill of the swimming team were distant memories. They both thought of themselves as outcasts, so different from everybody else.

Teachers, sympathetic to Mike because of the crash, awarded him good grades even though he did not earn them—ultimately, to Mike's detriment. Except for watching television, he had little interest in doing much of anything. He did not study hard any more. He was self-conscious about his frail and scarred appearance. In his wallet, Mike carried a vivid reminder of the crash—his Social Security card marred by a tiny drop of blood. He could not shake a feeling of melancholy. He could not understand why Roddy, Peachie and Sandy died, and he survived. Late at night, he was tormented by nightmares, waking up his father and the rest of the family with piercing screams. (18)

Mike sought out friends such as Janice Poplack, whose mother had died only a couple of years earlier. She seemed particularly sympathetic, one of the few people other than Bruce who could understand how he felt. Sometimes they went to a movie or walked about bustling Birmingham where kids were having the kind of fun that Mike, Roddy and Bruce once enjoyed.

One Saturday evening, Mike escorted Janice to a party at Orchard Lake Country Club. As he went through the motions of dancing with her, Mike saw his friends enjoying themselves. But Mike kept telling himself he shouldn't be there; he had no right to survive the accident. He was convinced that Janice was having a terrible time with him. He shouldn't be with her, he told himself. Why should he bring her down?

He drove Janice home in near silence. After he dropped her off, he turned his car onto Puritan toward his house. It was a narrow side street flanked by maple trees and dotted by an occasional parked car. He pressed the accelerator: Thirty, then 40 miles per hour in a 25-mile per hour zone. The well-lit colonial homes whizzed by, almost in a blur. He wanted to aim the car directly into a tree. Then he shook himself. He slowed down the car and drove home.

Bruce felt just as distant and lonely as Mike. As a Seaholm senior, Bruce studied relentlessly, earned a solid B average and qualified for Michigan State. But he quit the swimming team. He and Susie Martin broke up. When friends saw Bruce in the school hallway, he looked away, almost as if he felt everybody was staring at him.(19) He skipped the senior prom. In June, when the class of 1966 gathered in the school gymnasium for commencement, Bruce collected his diploma and avoided the parties afterward. Instead, he and Mike had lunch with their mothers at Orchard Lake Country Club.

Like Mike, he dreaded talking of that night in the Skylark. He told Bill Saefkow that the whole day had been wiped from his mind. When he took a make-up chemistry course during the summer, he saw an empty desk next to one of Sandy Christman's closest friends. "Do you mind if I sit here?" Bruce politely asked. He knew that she would be the only kid not to ask about the crash.(20) Butch Fleming thought the crash was "a real ugly subject" not to be discussed. Girls Bruce had known most of his life would invite Mike and Bruce over late at night to laugh and joke. But if anyone broached the subject of Roddy or the accident, Bruce grew silent. (21) During the summer, Bruce often worked part-time with his friend Dick Lowrie. They assembled swimming pools one year and the next year collected tolls from cars crossing the Ambassador Bridge that linked Detroit to Canada. But as much time as they spent together, Bruce never mentioned the accident.

Bruce only talked about the wreck when forced, and even then only fleetingly. When students in chemistry summer class conducted an experiment in hydrogen sulfide, they created a pungent odor similar to rotten eggs. Except for Bruce, the kids raced toward the open windows for fresh air. "I can't smell it," he told one girl. Then he laughed, "You wouldn't know." He had not told her that he did not have a sense of smell. (22)

Sure, he could avoid talking about the crash, but he could not stop thinking about it. He missed his close friend Roddy. When he

145

was alone, Bruce walked up Oak Street to the nearby cemetery and stood quietly before Roddy's grave. Roddy seemed indestructible, Bruce thought. He had been so special. He would have been an Olympic swimmer. How could anybody explain such a senseless end? One winter evening during his senior year, Bruce vanished from a group of friends. After a few minutes, they were puzzled. Then one of his buddies said, "I know where he is." They drove the short distance to the cemetery and eased past the iron gates. Mounds of snow flanked either side of the narrow road. The headlights illuminated Bruce, standing in the snow in front of his friend's headstone.

"I just came to see Roddy," he explained. (23)

The only people Mike and Bruce could truly be comfortable with were each other. They had been good friends since elementary school, but now there seemed a special bond between them. Bruce thought of themselves as "blood brothers almost." They hung out with other buddies–Dick Lowrie, Butch Fleming and Mark Morden. But throughout their senior year at Seaholm, Mike and Bruce were rarely apart, secure in the knowledge that neither would talk about the crash.

That spring, Bruce and Mike drove to New Orleans to visit a friend at Tulane University. They went through the motions of applying to Tulane, but were more interested in Bourbon Street. They went to a topless bar and managed to buy glasses of beer, even though Mike was only 17. A police officer demanded Mike's driver's license. "If you want to save yourselves some trouble, you'd better leave," the officer told them. Mike and Bruce nodded, waited for the officer to disappear and walked to another bar.(24)

It was the first time either ever remembered drinking a beer. Before the accident, Mike took a sip or two, but both avoided drinking, in large part because they immersed themselves in athletic training. But now that they had quit swimming, they liked a few beers. They weren't binge drinkers by any means, but Mike in particular could down a six-pack of Budweiser on a weekend night. They prevailed on Bruce's older brother to buy beer for them. A couple of times they drove to Pontiac and persuaded anyone they could find over age 21 to buy them beer.

Bruce gulped a beer as fast as he would a glass of water, although just two or three a night would make him woozy or giddy. Then to the amusement of friends, he would say something oddly funny, prompting them to respond with a catchy chorus: Mike would shrug, "He ain't my buddy." Another friend would chime in, "He ain't my pal." And a third would finish with, "He's no acquaintance of mine."

After a couple of beers, the quiet and shy Bruce displayed a more romantic, sentimental side. He talked about still having a crush on Susie Martin, who now was going steady with Mike. When Ken and Rita Berridge were out one night, Bruce, Dick Lowrie and Butch Fleming helped themselves to a few beers at the Berridge house. "I've got to see Susie," Bruce said. Don't be silly, they insisted. But Bruce had made up his mind. The three boys walked the short distance to her house, where Bruce tossed pebbles at her bedroom window and woke her up. They chattered away until Susie's father shooed them away. The next day, Bruce asked Lowrie, "What the hell have I done?" Susie was Mike Adair's girlfriend now, Bruce said. "I don't want to hurt my friend." (25)

Ken knew his son was drinking, but figured a few beers kept Bruce's mind from Roddy. One night Bruce passed out, forcing Butch Fleming and Dick Lowrie to take him home and quietly carry him upstairs to his bed. They tried to sneak out before waking anyone. But as they went downstairs, Ken was waiting. They were sure he was going to yell at them.

Instead, Ken surprised them: "Thanks fellows for taking care of Bruce. He needed that."(26)

Mike Adair continued to party and drink when he enrolled at Albion in the fall of 1966. He still talked of becoming a physician, but away from home for the first time in his life, he was too busy having a good time. He joined Delta Tau Delta, a fun-loving fraternity whose members earned the nickname "Downtown Drunks." His cousin Bob Adams, who also attended Albion, was puzzled. Mike nearly died because of a driver who drank and yet now had become just one of these "fun-loving, drinking college kids." Mike often made the drive over to Eastern Michigan University to party at Dick Lowrie's fraternity house. To Lowrie, Mike seemed so happy to just be alive that it was clear he "could care less about school."

During the summer of 1968, he and a buddy downed a few beers at Mike's house on Puritan. When the friend left to drive home, Mike pleaded with him to stay. You're too drunk to drive, Mike warned, but his friend shrugged him off. Mike jumped into his own car and screeched after his friend up Maple, passing the same drug store that Mike Drothler had when he roared down Maple from the opposite direction on that January night three years earlier. He was doing exactly what Mike Drothler had done. Then at 70 miles an hour, Mike darted up Lahser Road and down the sharp curves and sloping hills of Long Lake Road. When he reached his friend's house, he announced, "I just wanted to see if you were all right." Then, still drunk, Mike sped home.

His grades in college plummeted. Unlike his high school teachers, Mike's college professors displayed no special sympathy for him. Before the crash, Mike had been a solid B student and easily absorbed information from his textbooks. But now as he took demanding pre-medical courses, he groped his way through textbooks. He read a paragraph, paused for a moment, and then realized he forgot what he had just read. He tried again, forcing himself to concentrate. Once again after finishing the paragraph, he could not remember anything. Finally on the third or fourth or fifth try, he grasped what he had just read. He never mentioned it to anybody, but his frustration mounted and at times he tossed the books aside and grabbed a beer. By his junior year, Mike elected to take four challenging courses, including advanced physics, calculus and physical chemistry. He pushed himself to read and study; he wanted to become a physician and desperately hoped to achieve the grades necessary for medical school. But no matter how much time he devoted to study, his grades remained poor. In the middle of his junior year, he dropped out of college.

Mike did not realize it at the time, but the Albion failure was a result of the accident. When he smacked his head into the dashboard of the Skylark, he suffered a traumatic brain injury, which often prompts a personality change. The inability to remember what he just read was one sign, but there were others. He did not show initiative. He did not like talking about himself. He started projects, but rarely finished. He once took an electronics course, but after completing the schoolwork, lost interest in the subject. (27)

He returned home to Birmingham, to the house where he grew up. A town that once was so full of fun now seemed desolate. Roddy was dead, Bruce was doing well academically at Michigan State University, Dick Lowrie was at Eastern Michigan. He was alone with no idea what he wanted to do for a living.

Mike stopped by Beaumont–the same hospital where the ambulances brought all of them that night in 1965–and asked for a job in the laboratory. He was put to work analyzing urine samples and blood, work that appealed to his sense of actually doing something rather than just studying. He combined his full-time job with courses at Wayne State University. Every day, he boarded the bus to downtown Detroit and took classes for a degree in unified science and chemistry.

He met a young woman, Susan Watkins, who worked the Beaumont switchboard. Sue thought that with his curly brown hair, Mike bore a physical resemblance to actor Sal Mineo. She found his quiet style appealing. He asked a friend for her name and worked up the nerve to ask her out. They started dating in July 1969 – the same night the Apollo astronauts landed on the Moon.

At Michigan State, Bruce Berridge studied long hours, although during his first semester as a freshman he was disappointed in his grades. But determined to be a physician, he continued working hard, regularly earning solid Bs and achieving a perfect 4-point one semester. Unlike Mike, Bruce thrived on being away from Birmingham.

As a sophomore in 1967, he casually dated Sandy Christman's younger sister Donna, then a Michigan State freshman. They went to movies, danced with their friends or attended college parties. They did not talk about Sandy's death, but Bruce was sure one reason they dated was because "we were both suffering a little bit" from the crash. The crash remained a topic to be shunned. One close friend thought Bruce had finally put the crash behind him.

He became particularly close to his older brother Jim, who was at Michigan State too. He stayed close to a group of friends from Seaholm, including Dave Nelson, the backstroker who nearly joined Bruce and Roddy the night of the accident. Nelson, who years earlier surfed with Roddy in frigid Lake Huron, was always on the hunt for something fun, and Bruce usually tagged along. Late at night, they would climb the exterior of the tall smokestack over the university's massive power plant. When Nelson discovered a series of underground tunnels leading from the power plant to the rest of the university, he, Bruce and a few others snuck into one of them late at night, opened a manhole and exited on another side of campus. It was great fun until a worker at the power plant tipped off the police, who stationed officers at the exits. Sure enough, the manhole covers opened and up popped the boys, who were carted off to the police station.

"Whatever got you to do that?" an officer sternly asked. Bruce thought for a moment before replying, "Well, boys will be boys." The officers burst out laughing. (28)

By Bruce's senior year, he was seriously dating Georgine Bugor, a result of his close bond with Mike Adair. Susan Watkins had wanted to fix up Bruce with Georgine, a Michigan State senior who planned to teach school. Susan and Gina, as friends called her, grew up together and joked about having measles and chicken pox at the same time. Susan tried to arrange a date between Bruce and Gina, but one of them always seemed busy. "I'm not giving up," Susan told Gina. "One of these days, I'm going to get you on a blind date with one of Mike's friends." In December of 1970, Susan got lucky. She hosted a Christmas party at her apartment in Royal Oak and invited both Gina and Bruce. Gina instantly liked Bruce. By the following summer, they were dating regularly. (29)

As he entered his senior year, Bruce was torn between medical school and veterinary school. He grew ambivalent about medical school during a summer job at Henry Ford Hospital in Detroit. The physicians seemed brusque with their patients, which "turned him off" to medical school. Instead, armed with a degree in zoology, he applied at the veterinarian school at Michigan State—one of the strongest in the country. To his surprise, he was accepted. By his final year, he enjoyed veterinary school so much that he took courses during the day, worked at the animal clinic at night and lived in the intern quarters above the clinic where he and other students were on call through the night.

He had always loved animals. As a kid, he plucked dead squirrels from the street and buried them in his backyard, marking each grave with a cross. Now at the clinic, he learned new surgical techniques to keep animals alive. One afternoon, a young woman brought in a dog, which had been struck by a car. When the vets told her the surgery would cost $700, she suggested they "put him to sleep." The students shaved the dog, inserted a steel rod in his back, stitched him back together and placed him in one of the cages downstairs. When Bruce saw the dog, which seemed a cross between a poodle and a schnauzer, he took a liking to him. So Bruce adopted the dog, surgically removed the steel rod and named him "Ollie."

Ollie, Gina joked, was "the one love of his life." On a bitterly cold winter day, Bruce and Gina took Ollie for a walk near the Cedar River on the Michigan State campus. A large sign proclaimed that dogs were not allowed in the park, but Bruce removed Ollie's leash and let him run. Ollie saw a bird and dashed on to the frozen river, and when the ice broke, tumbled into the water. In horror, Bruce watched as Ollie tried in vain to climb back on to the ice.

Bruce turned to Gina. "I can't let him die."

He removed his winter jacket and gingerly made his way across the frozen river. When he was a few feet away from Ollie, the ice shattered and Bruce plunged into the water up to his waist. A large piece of ice separated Bruce from Ollie. Bruce slapped the ice with his right arm until it cracked. The jagged ice slashed his arm, but he grasped Ollie and waded back to shore. Bruce carried Ollie to his Volkswagen, sat in the passenger seat and tried to dry off the shivering dog.

"You're going to have to drive," Bruce told Gina.

"I don't know how to drive a stick," Gina protested.

"You do the steering," Bruce answered. "I'll shift." They drove to Gina's apartment, where Bruce tenderly dried Ollie with a towel. He bandaged his own bleeding arm and got a Tetanus shot. But Ollie was safe.(30)

When Mike Adair married Susan Watkins in March of 1971, he asked Bruce Berridge to be best man. A year earlier, Bruce served as best man at Dick Lowrie's wedding, but he dreaded the thought of delivering a toast. So he drank a couple of beers and said, "I hope Dick and Barb are happy." Then he turned to the guests and said, "Mom, how did I do?" To Mike, it was enough to start the refrain, "He ain't my buddy."(31)

Once again at Mike's wedding, Bruce had to deliver a toast at the rehearsal dinner at Orchard Lake Country Club. He confessed to friends that he did not have the vaguest idea what to say. "Oh just say whatever comes into your mind," one friend told him. Bruce thought for a moment and decided the only thing he knew about was a class he had just taken on animal digestion. He solemnly stood and proceeded to discuss the end of the digestive tract of a dog. The guests burst into applause and laughter. (32)

For Mike, marriage to Susan, like college at Albion, did not take. Susan's parents were dead, and Mike's sisters privately suspected that was one reason he'd been attracted to her. Susan was one of the few people who could understand the trauma haunting Mike. They had a daughter Jessica and a son Robin. Mike doted on both. Susan liked Mike's generous nature, but she detected signs that Mike had not come to grips with the crash and the death of his friends. She was certain he had suffered some form of a brain injury. She finally persuaded him to see a marriage counselor, but after the first session Mike announced, "There's nothing wrong with me, and I'm not going to change anything."(33)

Mike's struggles were particularly difficult for his father. Like Jack Barnum, Dr. Adair was obsessed with the accident. Late one evening shortly after the crash, Nancy Adair found him sitting alone in the darkened living room, illuminated only by a few dying logs in the fireplace. He could not sweep away the horror of that night, his battered son and the realization that Mike nearly died. He had to endure Mike's agonizing screams from his nightmares. There was Mike's poor performance at Albion. Dr. Adair had trouble talking about the crash to Betty, so often he confided in his oldest daughter Sue. The crash had a "devastating" impact on Mike's life, Dr. Adair told her. Sue suggested Mike be sent to a therapist, but nothing ever came of the idea. (34)

In September of 1976, Dr. Adair felt a sharp pain in his chest while delivering a baby at St. Joseph Hospital in Pontiac. He handed the baby to a nurse, crumpled to the floor and died. He was just two months away from his 61st birthday. The official cause was a heart attack, but his friends knew the accident "took the starch out of him." (35)

For Mike, his father's death was but another in a series of blows that left him bewildered. Nothing seemed to be going right for him. A few years later, Beaumont officials eliminated his job analyzing blood. They offered him a job as a hospital security guard. As a kid, Mike wanted to be a physician at a modern hospital, just like his father. Now, at the age of 34, he was told the best he could hope for was a security job. By 1981, Mike was jobless and collecting unemployment, his marriage in tatters.

Every day, he thought of the crash, of Roddy, Peachie and Sandy. But he never linked the black Galaxie to his inability to graduate from Albion, attend medical school and become a doctor. Instead, he blamed himself. He was a failure, he told himself. Worse, he had let his dad down.

TEN

"Who is Nancy?"

Krisa Barnum was astonished: More than 150 people packed into a banquet hall in Southfield that day in 1972, good friends and business associates of Jack Barnum's who wanted to celebrate his retirement from IBM and say goodbye. At 56, Jack walked away from the company where he'd spent a quarter of a century. Telling people he wouldn't live much longer, Jack wanted to move to Florida to recapture the happiness he found there as a torpedo bomber pilot. The Barnum sisters hoped that by leaving Birmingham, Jack and Betty could escape the memory of their dead daughter, and perhaps start a new life while both were young enough to enjoy themselves. Krisa had always assumed that Jack's gruff and demanding style had turned off everybody at IBM. But instead she listened in rapt attention to glowing speeches in which his subordinates credited Jack for bringing out the best in them.(1)

Krisa, now a high school student, moved with her parents to Naples, Florida, where Jack bought a boat, named it the *Krisa* and seemed to achieve some semblance of happiness for a time. After years of resisting pleas from his daughters, Jack consented to move Peachie's casket from the crypt in a Birmingham-area cemetery to a burial plot. He reconciled with Jacquey, although it took intricate stage directions from Betty. Jacquey, by now an event planner with a major insurance company in Chicago, flew to Florida on a business trip. She telephoned her mother who pleaded with Jacquey to visit.

"It's time," Betty told her. "You have to deal with your father."

Krisa could see her father making the effort to develop a relationship with her. Every day she raced home from high school to watch the TV show "Jeopardy" with her dad. The night before she attended her first class at Florida State University, they stayed up much of the night and talked. Jack told her about meeting in 1942 with the wives of the dead pilots and tail-gunners of Torpedo

Squadron 8; how tortuous it was to explain why their husbands weren't coming home.

Krisa spent two years at Florida State, detesting every minute of it. But when she planned to transfer to a community college in Gainesville, Jack was furious. You made a four-year commitment, he said, and transferring showed a lack of discipline. But Krisa had her way, and completed courses in paralegal work, joking to friends that she earned a degree in "underwater basket weaving and roach clips." She landed a job as a paralegal, but was bored. Instead of quitting, she wrote a memo to her boss, urging him to re-organize his office. By taking a few simple steps, Krisa wrote, the attorney could save money by cutting his staff in half, including eliminating her job. Rather than rewarding Krisa for initiative, the attorney took her advice. He fired her.

Jack thought Krisa's outgoing personality would be perfect for sales, so he arranged an interview at IBM. The thought of entering her father's field appealed to Krisa if for no other reason than to prove to him she wasn't an "idiot." Particularly after the accident, Krisa sensed that her father thought she wasn't very serious; he often suggested she was immature. "Well, I'm going to show him," Krisa vowed. Her interview at IBM went well, until she was asked about her career goals. She announced, "Well, if I like it, I'd like to be president." Such brashness did not sit well at buttoned-down IBM. (2)

So she went to work for Memorex, which was selling high-speed tapes. She performed so well, that she was recruited to be the first woman to sell mainframe computers for Digital in suburban Detroit. Krisa was delighted. Not only was she advancing in her father's field, the move allowed her to leave Florida's humid weather.

Much to her surprise, she discovered she was more like Jack than she ever realized, that the "acorn didn't fall far from the tree." Like her dad was before Peachie's death, Krisa could be a "crack-up." She worked hard, becoming as addicted to work as Jack had once been. She won a promotion and a transfer to Boston, where she earned a handsome salary, managed an office of men and women and bought a condominium outside the city. She borrowed $5,000 from Jack for the down payment, and, in his typical fashion, he insisted she pay it back with interest. He even had his attorney insert a clause in his will requiring Krisa to repay the loan.(3)

Even though she no longer lived with her father, Krisa knew he was struggling emotionally. Following a near boating accident, he sold the boat. He stopped playing golf and did not have any hobbies to occupy him. Jack was increasingly moody. He smoked too many cigarettes and drank too much vodka. He rarely spoke to anyone about Peachie, and if the topic came up, nobody could say anything that would comfort him. He could not understand why such a terrible accident took his daughter away. (4)

When Betty developed the early stages of Alzheimer's at age 57, the disease overwhelmed Jack. He simply could not handle the day-to-day burden of caring for Betty, so Jacquey, Patty and Krisa moved her into a nursing home near Patty's home in Chicago. Every day, Patty visited. During Christmas of 1984, Patty and Jacquey took turns feeding their mother with a spoon. In the winter of 1985, Jack found himself alone in Naples. He dreaded the idea of ending his life in a nursing home. He told his daughters that after his death, they should toss his ashes over the side of a boat.

Nobody ever thought Jack would end up so gloomy. On the eve of his wedding in 1943, his grandmother Nan composed a poem that reflected so much about Jack:

"You have won honors in battle,
You courageously risked your life.
Another honor you have won,
  in choosing a wonderful wife.
Always so efficient—true blue,
  Then your commission has ended,
There will be much in store for you."

In early 1985, Jack decided to visit each daughter. He arrived in Boston to see Krisa at the height of winter and was shocked at the

157

biting cold. Years later, Krisa regretted not taking time off from work to be with her father, but just like Jack, she was a workaholic. After Krisa went to work every morning, Jack would wrap himself in a ski jacket, turn the condominium's heat up to 90 and grumble, "It's fucking cold out there." He seemed to enjoy himself, though, especially when Krisa and her boyfriend took him out to dinner. Thinking that Krisa might marry the guy, Jack turned to him and said, "You're going to take care of her. Right?" Typically for Jack, it was a command, not a request.(5)

A few months after dinner with Krisa and feeling ill, Jack checked himself into a hospital near his Naples' home. Jacquey, Patty and Krisa flew to Florida. They went through his car, still parked in the hospital lot, and discovered two cases of vodka in the trunk. They moved Jack to a convalescent home. On an April day in 1985, Jack complained to Jacquey that he was suffering from a head cold. When she called the next day, Jack was coughing so badly she was certain he had pneumonia. Alarmed, she called the convalescent home twice the next day. Finally that evening, Jack was moved to a hospital and the three sisters flew to Naples.

"Your father has gone into a coma," the doctor explained. The sisters walked into the hospital room where Jack was connected to a machine. He was breathing softly. Their father had always made it clear he did not want to be kept alive by some machine. They asked the doctors and nurses to leave the room for a few minutes. They sang the "Barnum girls" jingle they made up years ago when Peachie was alive and Jack was soaring at IBM. Then they told the doctors to disconnect Jack from the machine.

Nine months later on April 13, 1986, Betty died. It would have been Jack's 70th birthday. They held a service for Jack and Betty at White Chapel, the cemetery where Peachie was buried. A large crowd gathered in the first-floor chapel. Krisa was overwhelmed to see one of her supervisors in the chapel. Sandy Christman's younger sister Linda was there. The Barnum sisters stood before the mourners and held the aging hardcover book of poetry written by Jack's grandmother, which she published half-a-century earlier. They each read one selection:

"The leaf must die, the flower fall,
To make the fallow earth,
But at the voice of nature's call,
We soon observe a glorious birth."

It did not matter what Jack's death certificate said, Krisa and her sisters knew better: Jack died of a broken heart. He had been killed by the black Galaxie as surely as if he had been in the Skylark with Peachie, Roddy, and Sandy. Krisa recognized that anybody even remotely connected to the accident had "huge scars that completely warped our lives." She was determined that would not happen to her. Within days after her father's death, she telephoned a therapist.

By the late 1970s, Nancy Henderson and her brother Jim were both working for Business News, their father's company. When Jim joined the company in 1969, his daily presence injected Ed with fresh enthusiasm. Still innovative, Ed bought a computer in 1970 and followed with a $400 hand-held calculator, which was passed around the office for everyone to use. He moved the company to nearby Troy, an expanding, vibrant area not far from uptown Birmingham. He was proud of the office. Once again, Ed sought ways to expand his company, rooting about to buy an office building or publish a few books.(6)

While Jim was groomed to eventually manage the company, Nancy focused on writing articles or helping design the magazine. In 1979, she left her small apartment in Birmingham. She and a girlfriend shared a bigger two-bedroom apartment near Somerset Mall in Troy. She volunteered once a week for a local hotline as a counselor. She rode horses, cross-country skied, and flew to Aspen for vacations and downhill skiing.

She and a close group of girlfriends prowled for guys at area bars, particularly Hurley's in the Hilton Hotel on Crooks Road. There they sat at one of the tables, hoisted drinks for long hours and chatted and danced with the men who flocked around them. Now in her late 20s, Nancy looked radiant and easily attracted men. One evening she met a guy who had known Roddy and was glad when he called her for a date. She dated a lot, but also drank a lot—too much, in her mind. For her 28th birthday in 1979, three of her girlfriends took her out for drinks at Hurley's. The next morning, her head felt like it had been smacked with a rock and she was late to work. Never again, she vowed to herself, writing in her diary, "I've thought about it all and have wondered what has brought me to all this. I'm a mess."(7) Yet she continued to party with her friends and drive herself home after drinking too much. She wrote about drinking and driving in her diary, but in her writings, she never linked it to Roddy's death.

She was eager to find a man who could simultaneously offer a romantic relationship and yet fill the void left by Roddy. Yet whenever she became involved in a happy relationship, she would be filled with anxiety, fearful that any important romance would end badly. In the summer of 1979, she dated a man who lived nearby. On an unusually cool August evening, she walked over to his apartment and poured out her fears. "I feel so good about our relationship," she told him. But that scared her because she couldn't stand "the thought of losing someone again." She was convinced that if she truly enjoyed her life and the man she was with, all would be snatched away in an instant, just as Roddy was. At times, she found that only alcohol could soothe those demons.(8)

There was a brief marriage in 1980, a poor choice she realized. When it ended in 1982, Nancy fled Birmingham to start fresh. She drove to San Francisco where a couple of old girl friends lived, but after a few days, moved on to Aspen. She leased a two-room condo at the base of Aspen Mountain and next to the Roaring Fork River, arranged to have her furniture shipped from Michigan and tried to land a magazine job. When that failed, she worked as a nanny for a wealthy Aspen family. She ran across an acquaintance from Oakland Hills Country Club who had known Roddy; he became one of her few friends in Aspen.

During the Christmas holidays of 1982, she was so dejected that she didn't bother to get a tree. On Christmas Day, a friend stopped by, but after he left, she drifted off to sleep on her living room couch. She awoke the next morning still on the couch, having never made it to her bedroom. On New Year's Eve, Nancy walked into the village to have a drink with a couple of friends, but left before midnight to return alone to her condo. There she stood outside and watched the fireworks explode above Aspen Mountain.

Hoping to wipe away her gloomy mood, she flew to San Francisco in the spring of 1983 for a vacation, only to have a thief swipe her purse and suitcase. Gone were her amethyst ring, driver's license, credit cards, Social Security card, keys, address book with friends' phone numbers and a journal that contained a full year of diary entries. In despair, she scribbled in a new journal, "Who is Nancy? This is the ultimate. I lost all ID. I have no identity, not even a piece of paper." She flew back to Aspen and let herself into her condominium, using a spare key she had wisely hidden at the building. Alone in her living room, she munched on popcorn and drank wine until she dozed off.(9)

Her life had turned out so differently than the one she imagined as a kid. Her bleak diary entries that spring of 1983 were a stark contrast to the notations before Roddy's accident. In September of 1964, she wrote elatedly about attending a Beatles' concert in Detroit: "I don't think I've ever heard or done so much screaming in my entire life." The week before the crash, she dashed off an entry about a swimming meet between Barnum and Derby. Her girlfriend was going steady with a Derby swimmer, but after the meet the swimmer thrilled Nancy by paying so much attention to her. As Nancy leaned against the doorway of the Barnum cafeteria, the Derby swimmer flirtatiously teased, "I'll bet you were just planning for me to walk by and trip over that foot." Not a bad idea, Nancy jokingly replied.(10) Her schedule as a kid had been so crowded: Fun-packed sleepovers at her girlfriend's house; horseback riding at Arrowhead Ranch, and snow skiing at Alpine Valley with her closest girlfriends the day after New Year's in 1965, where they checked out "lots of cute guys." As a

13-year-old, she was alone only when she chose to be, to write poetry or play her guitar. Now, in Aspen, a virtual paradise for everyone else, she was desperately isolated. "I gaze at the child I used to be," she would later write. "She seems like someone else now."(11) Too often she sat alone in her apartment and wept. "The days are so long and empty," she wrote in her diary. (12)

Like Mike Adair, she seemed lost after the accident. Unlike him, she knew why. The day before the crash, she was so happy. The next evening, everything changed forever.

She missed her old job at Business News and her friends in Birmingham. Even though she wasn't sure she truly belonged in Michigan, she knew Aspen was not right either. She had lived through so much–Roddy's death, searching for a man to replace her brother, drinking too much wine–that she felt like "such an old lady." In reality, she was only 32 and was as lovely as ever.

Nancy knew she had to go home again. She called a moving company to ship her furniture, and carefully packed her dishes and clothes. On an April afternoon in 1983, she eased into the front seat of her car. By 4:30 in the afternoon, she had reached Denver, where it was snowing. She continued to the Nebraska state line. It was dark and heavy rain pounded the highway. Exhausted, she rented a hotel room and for the first time in days slept soundly, free from her persistent nightmares. The next night, she was in Iowa, where she slept in a hotel and arose at 6 a.m. for the final lap home. Then east on Interstate 94, the four-lane freeway that linked Chicago to Detroit. By six in the evening, she was on Southfield Road, the artery that led toward uptown Birmingham. She turned west on Maple Road, past Quarton Lake and up the hill to Henderson's Light. She thought of Roddy, as she always did when she passed the curve and the light. A few minutes later, she was at her parents' home on Westwood, where she had a long talk with Ed and Helen, ate a light snack, unpacked her suitcases and flopped into bed in her old room.

In the coming weeks, she leased an apartment near the Somerset Mall, re-connected with good friends, took a job in advertising at Business News and checked out the class schedules at Oakland

Community College, where she took courses in art and photography. Preferring to be involved in production, she left Business News for another company that produced automotive publications. She began seeing a therapist again. On a quiet evening at the end of April, she listened to the birds chirping, gazed at new leaves forming on the trees and saw that the forsythias and magnolias were blooming. She had made so many mistakes, she thought. She wanted to change her life, she wanted to be happy. She thought she was making a good beginning. (13)

Nancy returned to find her father still obsessed with keeping busy. But no matter how outwardly busy Ed was, he was haunted by the loss of his gifted son. After playing golf at Oakland Hills one afternoon with Ed, Corey Van Fleet thought that the memory of Roddy was as fresh to Ed as the night of the accident. Roddy's friends could see the same thing. "He never got over it," one said. "It changed his life." (14)

Ed had always suffered from a sensitive stomach and in 1983, surgeons removed a stomach tumor. He seemed to recover and as late as January of 1986 was snow skiing in Gaylord. A few months later, however, physicians discovered a slow-growing malignant tumor in his liver. By October, he was so weak that Helen temporarily moved him to a hospice. Physicians changed his medicine and stabilized him so he could eat and sleep. They sent him back home where Helen installed a hospital bed in Jim's old room.

Ed's sense of humor was gone. When he was lucid, he alternated between bouts of anger and despair, once telling Nancy that he just wanted to die. He was so disoriented that a nurse had to tell him that Nancy was in the room. Ed grasped his daughter's hand, repeated her name and said, "I won't get to know you."(15)

Four days later after a sleepless night in her own apartment, Nancy made plans to visit Ed. But as she started to dress, the phone rang.

"It's over," Helen said. It was 9:10 in the morning of November 14, 1986.

They arranged for friends to see Ed at the same Birmingham funeral home where Roddy had been two decades ago. The room was awash with flowers. More than 150 people signed a guest registry: Colleagues at Business News; old golfing buddies; new friends he made with ham radio, and Corey Van Fleet. Roddy's friend Mark Morden visited. Bruce Berridge and Gina sent a handwritten card. Mike Adair and his mom Betty walked in. Nancy was glad; she had not seen Mike in years.

The next day there was a service at the First Methodist Church on Maple Road, where Helen Henderson worshiped every Sunday. There was a short drive to the same cemetery where Roddy and his grandmother were buried. The pallbearers carried the casket to a freshly dug grave next to Roddy's. A minister spoke briefly. Nancy and Jim hosted a reception. When the last guest departed, they returned to the cemetery. It was bitterly cold. Snow fell from the gray sky. Nancy straightened out the flowers next to her father's grave. A solitary Mum had broken free from the arrangement. Nancy scooped up the flower and placed it in front of Roddy's headstone. (16)

Ed's death marked another passage in Nancy's reassessment of her own life. She would soon be 36 years old. She wanted to grow up and stop feeling sorry for herself over so many things–her brother's death, her first marriage, her own life. "The past is gone, over with–there's nothing I can do about it," she wrote in her diary. (17)

"OK, I've got to clean up my life," she thought.

She vowed to stop drinking, entered a rehabilitation clinic for one month, and never drank again. Her father's will provided her with money to buy a house, a welcome change after years of renting apartments. She selected a "cute little" two-bedroom house in Birmingham close to 14-Mile Road and Woodward. It was small – with a first-floor bedroom she used as an office and an upstairs loft with a bedroom. Because it was only four years old, most of the appliances and fixtures worked perfectly. She painted the house a stylish beige, re-landscaped the back and front yards, hung wallpaper and curtains, cleaned the furnace, added a humidifier and installed cable for her two television sets. There was a wooden deck out back where on summer evenings she relaxed in a white-painted iron chair. "I love this house," she wrote on a Halloween evening that was so cold it seemed more like Christmas. "I could just exist in this house for the rest of my life and be perfectly happy. I've gained 10 pounds. I have no desire to drink and never will." (18)

She saw a therapist and talked about Roddy. When Roddy was killed, Nancy told the therapist, she became the focus of the Henderson household. Jim was at Michigan State and Nancy was the only child left at home. She felt pressure to excel in school and athletics, to be every bit as accomplished as Roddy, and to do so at a time when she was emotionally ravaged by his death. But she was sure she could never equal Roddy, who found it so easy to make friends and so easy to conquer life. She lacked Roddy's competitive zeal and concluded that she did not know how to be good at anything—whether training horses, earning good grades or developing a relationship with a man. Now as she looked back on her life, she understood why at times she seemed so aimless. (19)

Nancy found a job in Southfield at a picture framing shop, a task she enjoyed because it was so creative. "Things are shaping up pretty well," she wrote. "I'm happy. I'm doing everything—a little bit of everything. I'm going to be pretty busy, but it feels good."(20) There was a new guy and they enjoyed sailing on Lake St. Clair. There was a trip to the Mediterranean to visit friends on an island off the Spanish coast. Every year, she flew to New Mexico to hike in the mountains, shop for Native American pottery and snap photographs of the adobe buildings with their colorful turquoise doors and trim.

Yearning to find an outlet for her creativity, in the winter of 1992 Nancy enrolled in a creative writing class at the Community House in uptown Birmingham. At her first writing class, she listened to the others in the course read their poetry and essays. Soon she read her own poetry to the class and quickly realized, "this is what I was meant to do." (21)

As a kid, she had written her poetry to rhyme, but now she evolved to a more sophisticated free-verse style. She particularly admired the work of Pulitzer Prize poet Mary Oliver—"Whoever you are, no matter how lonely, the world offers itself to your imagination." She loved reading William Stafford's "You Must Revise Your Life," a book of essays about writing poetry. She was accepted into a graduate program in creative writing at Antioch University in Ohio, which allowed her to work on a master's degree while living in Birmingham. She attended writing workshops in South Carolina, New Mexico, Oregon and Minneapolis, where she met Natalie Goldberg, the author and writing coach who helped writers overcome their fears of being criticized and rejected.

While attending one writing conference in western Michigan, she stayed overnight in a hotel. Once again, her sleep was interrupted by a nightmare: She wrecked her car. Roddy was there with a girl, and Nancy asked her brother to help get the car repaired. Roddy refused, telling Nancy he needed to fix his own car. She started to walk for help. She cried. Then she woke up. It was daylight, she realized. Roddy was gone, she told herself. She had loved him, but he had his selfish side. Had he lived, she thought, perhaps he would not have helped her make decisions or deal with her life. Maybe life would have turned out exactly the same for her, with or without Roddy. She had to survive on her own.(22)

The facilitator of her writing group invited her to join other women to publish two books of their poetry and fiction. Nancy thought of writing as "a process that leads me to create meaning." The memory of Roddy, his seemingly inexplicable death and her years of agony and recovery seeped into her poetry. "Her brother, a smile in her childhood, will never make it past sixteen," she wrote. She described Roddy's funeral and the friends and neighbors who came to the house, not knowing what words could console the Hendersons. "I walk down the stairs of my childhood home into a room full of small talk. People talk to fill the air . . . But small talk is easier than answers."(23)

In August of 1994, she began a poem that would explain the fear that haunted her for years and led to her drinking: Enjoy life and it would all end, as abruptly as Roddy's had. She harked back to one of her favorite pop songs from the summer of 1967, Van Morrison's

"Brown Eyed Girl." She sat on a couch in her living room, and, grasping a pen and spiral notebook, wrote verses. The words came quickly. She crossed out only a few phrases, fidgeted with others. When she was satisfied, she typed the poem on a computer, edited and printed it, and read it to her writing group. They made a few suggestions, and a week later, she joined the group again for another reading. Ten women sat around a large dining room table in a suburban home with its view of thick woods. They sipped hot tea, coffee and bottled water. Nancy put on her glasses and in an even voice read the 33 lines. The room was quiet. When she finished, one woman asked her about a particular line—"The future could be gone in a second, like my brother was." What happened to your brother, she asked? Nancy explained. You need to say that, the women told her. Nancy scrawled the word, "More," on her paper. After she drove back home, she changed the phrase to read: "The future could be gone in a second, like my brother was, in his burgundy Skylark." There was no need, she thought, to explain any further. One week later, surrounded by the same women at the same dining room table, she read through the final version. The poem's last line was from Van Morrison's song:

"I drive down Woodward at dusk
with Van Morrison's 'Brown-Eyed Girl'
transporting me back to sixteen
when I drove up and down Woodward
looking for boys. My eyes are green, but I knew the song
was about me. I believed today
was the only day. The future
could be gone in a second,
like my brother was, in his
burgundy Skylark. I traveled
each day enclosed in a fog
of uncertainty that time
was inconsequential. Certain
if I really lived,

life would be taken away.
What is it like? To suddenly
not be able to drive down Woodward at dusk,
to not be able to hear 'Brown-Eyed Girl.'
Where does the music go?
My soul cannot exist
without the waves of song
that follow even in silence.
At forty-three, I know
I have been here too long
to believe the music will leave me,
to believe I shouldn't live
just because it may be taken away.
Here, I float on asphalt, contented
with who I have become, securing
that song in my memory . . .
believing I will stay with this music . . .
longer . . . overcome thinkin' about it."(24)

ELEVEN

"A time to heal"

It was a month before Mike Adair's second wedding in 1987. The minister was going over the details of the ceremony with Mike and his fiancée Connie Hydrick. The wedding would be held in May in a large church in Grand Rapids, a cream-colored brick structure of English Gothic design built in 1868, complete with bell tower and Tiffany stained glass windows. Connie grew up in Grand Rapids and had selected the church for their wedding–a church where she had been baptized and attended throughout the years with her family. Just 50 guests were invited–the couple's family and best friends. Mike would wear a gray business suit. Connie opted for a cream-colored suit. After the wedding, there would be a reception at a restaurant in an old Grand Rapids estate. Then Mike and Connie would cap off the day with an intimate dinner with a few close friends.

As the minister finished the plans with Mike and Connie, he mentioned they had not selected any Scripture to be read during the ceremony. "Do either of you have any preference?" he asked. Mike remembered those days so long ago when he was recovering from surgery in Houston, and the radio continually played the Byrds' new hit, "Turn, Turn, Turn." The lyrics, adapted by Pete Seeger from Ecclesiastes, had struck Mike as particularly poignant–"A time to be born, a time to die; A time to plant, a time to reap; A time to kill, a time to heal." For the next two decades, Mike often dwelled on those lyrics: His best friends had been killed. He and Bruce barely survived. He failed at Albion and lost his job at Beaumont. The memory of the accident crushed the life from his father. He never understood how much his father suffered until he became a parent. As he watched his 18-month-old daughter Jessica playing in the front yard in the spring of 1975, he thought, "If anything ever happened to her . . . " It struck him that the real victims of the crash had been the parents.(1)

Now, Mike told the minister, it was time for him to heal and he wanted to use the lyrics from the song.

"We don't usually use that in weddings," the minister replied. "But maybe that is something that appeals to you."

The wedding ceremony a month later went off flawlessly; those who knew Mike understood the words. Mike believed he had escaped the accident's grasp on his life. He loved living with Connie, kept in close touch with his best friends from Seaholm and Albion, played golf throughout the summer and joined college buddies for Detroit Tigers' baseball games downtown. He had a job analyzing blood samples at Henry Ford Hospital. If he couldn't be a doctor, at least he was involved in medicine.

But after dinner that night in the Grand Amway Hotel, the stomach pain that had plagued him since the accident flared up once more. He choked so much that a frightened Connie thought he was going to asphyxiate. She telephoned her father, a physician, and they met him at a nearby emergency room. (2)

For years, Mike had lived with the searing heartburn. Once after lunch with his cousin Bob Adams, his stomach throbbed, his shoulder ached and he was breathing heavily. Mike was certain the pain was from the auto accident, but Adams feared Mike was having a heart attack and drove him to Beaumont Hospital. During the ride, Mike kept his customary sense of humor. If he died, Mike jokingly said, he wanted Bob to have his golf clubs. Physicians did a cardiac catherization, and to everyone's relief, Mike's heart was fine, the Dacron in his aorta as solid as ever. But the intense heartburn always came back. It hurt so much when he lay down at night, he propped himself up with stacks of pillows, creating a hospital bed at home. Swimming, in particular, aggravated his heartburn. He would guzzle Maalox, jump in the pool at Henry Ford Hospital and put himself through a grueling workout.

To Connie, drinking Maalox and propping up pillows was no answer. "Something has to be done about this," Connie told her father. She contacted a specialist at the University of Michigan. Toward the end of 1987, the doctor delivered the bad news: For the fifth time because of the accident, Mike needed surgery. The surgeons at Michigan cut through the same scar Dr. Cooley sliced through two decades earlier. The doctors wrapped Mike's stomach around the esophagus and created a one-way valve. Food could get into his stomach, but nothing could go up. As the surgeons worked, Betty Adair sat in the waiting room with Connie. Betty harked back to the auto crash. It seemed there was always something, this time the stomach ailment, pulling her son back to that night in 1965. (3)

Yet this time, after five operations and more than 20 years, Mike was finally beginning to move forward, in ways major and minor. Within a few months of the operation, he was golfing with a college friend and shot one-over par for nine holes. He took up scuba diving. He and Connie bought a brick center-hall colonial off Woodward Avenue in Pleasant Ridge, just a few miles south of Birmingham. The stomach pains were a thing of the past. His face had completely healed, and nobody would have guessed that he had been in a major car crash. Once during a physical exam, a doctor poked at the scars on Mike's chest. Mike told him about the ruptured aorta and the subsequent surgery in Houston. The disbelieving doctor replied, "You can't live through that."(4) But Mike had done exactly that. There were many reasons: His plucky optimism, his sense of what really mattered in life, his compulsive determination to stay close to old friends. All helped him survive from those first days in the hospital so long ago.

He could still recall the young girl who visited him while he was recovering from the car crash. She faced the prospect of kidney dialysis the rest of her life or even of dying, and yet she seemed so upbeat. If she can handle it, Mike thought, so can I.

Some of those close to him believed one major reason he recovered was his unbreakable connections to old friends. In turn, Mike's wife Connie was certain that "something connected to the accident" propelled him to keep friends so close. Once Mike developed a friendship, he never wanted to lose that connection. After Eddie Watkins' mother died in 1993, Mike showed up for the service even though he had not seen Eddie since 1972. Eddie was touched.

When Sue Melcher was going through a divorce with Mark Morden, Mike called her. "Hey Melcher," Mike Adair said without bothering to introduce himself. He would be in the Seaholm gym tomorrow, watching Jessica play volleyball, Mike told her. Because Sue worked in the principal's office, it would be a convenient place to meet. The next day, she walked into the Seaholm gym and sat down next to Mike on one of the bleachers. "Why didn't you tell me?" he asked. She explained that because Mike, Roddy, Bruce and Mark had all been so close, she didn't want to put Mike in the position of taking sides.

"I'm both of your friends," Mike answered.(5)

More than anything, Mike had no desire to be alone. He played golf regularly with old friends from Albion. He met John Allman for lunch, stayed in contact with Dick Lowrie and often joined his cousin Bob Adams at the Red Coat Tavern on Woodward Avenue for the Red Coat Special, a thick hamburger with lettuce and a signature sauce. He and Eddie Watkins, who had lived in San Diego since 1966, made a point of playing golf every summer, either at the Birmingham Country Club or at a resort near Traverse City. Watkins would fly in, and Mike would dutifully collect him from Metropolitan Airport for a weekend of golf. When Watkins' father became ill in the late 1990s, Eddie often flew home to Michigan. Virtually every time, Mike would be waiting at the airport. (6)

A Seaholm class re-union in 1995 allowed Mike to re-connect with even more old friends—Janice Poplack, Nancy Ackerly, Bill Canning and Susie Martin. Mike always seemed to know where everybody was, even though he never kept an address book. It was, Mike joked, "just all up in my brain." Bill Crandell, who swam with Mike in junior high school, marveled at Mike's ability to know virtually every detail about old friends' lives. "If Mike ever gets to know you, he will know all about you," Crandell said.

Still the jokester, Mike enjoyed answering to two names. His high school friends, mother, brothers and sisters called him Mike. His college friends referred to him by his first name, Robin. His first wife Sue called him Mike; Connie called him Robin. Sometimes, he seemed a bit confused. Once when he telephoned Nancy Ackerly, he identified himself as Robin. Then he quickly realized Nancy was a friend from high school. "Nance, wait. This is Mike."(7) The two names gave him a chance to joke about the black Galaxie. If anyone wondered if he suffered brain damage in the crash, he would crack, "It depends on who you ask."

If Mike's salvation was to keep old friends close, Bruce Berridge's was to put distance between himself and Birmingham. During his final year of veterinary school at Michigan State, Bruce could have worked for a veterinarian hospital just a couple of miles from his home in Birmingham. But he hesitated. He was sure his mother's friends would bring all their pets to him and say, "There's little Brucie." Maybe now was the time to move, either to California or the East Coast. "For the first year, let's be adventuresome," he told Gina. "If we don't like it where we are, we can always come back." By leaving Michigan, he could start over and avoid the constant reminders of the accident. He did not want to keep visiting Roddy's grave or dwell on the black Galaxie. Where Mike thought about the crash everyday and Nancy Henderson spoke of it in therapy and poetry, Bruce Berridge wanted nothing to do with it. With his steely determination, he pushed it out of his mind and focused on his career and family.

On a bulletin board in the lower level of the veterinary school, Bruce spied a posting for a job in Boston with an animal clinic. During spring break, he flew to Boston to see the clinic near Cambridge, home to Harvard University and MIT. The hospital was something of a shock. Its grungy appearance was a marked contrast to the clean and immaculate hospitals he had seen as a student. But he accepted the job even though it meant long hours at $12,000 a year. He spent a weekend searching for an apartment that would allow him to keep Ollie and settled on a small rental on the top floor of a three-story building. A week later, Gina and her father drove Bruce's car from Michigan. Her father, horrified at the decrepit apartment, told Bruce he would pay for them to move to a better building.

At first, they both missed Michigan and spoke of returning. Bruce and Gina flew to Birmingham in August of 1973 to get married. Helen Henderson gave Gina a wedding shower, and Mike Adair was in the wedding party. But Michigan was in the grips of an economic slowdown caused by spiking oil prices, and Bruce and Gina thought the time was not right to go back home. After a second year in Boston, they liked it so much they chose to stay. Bruce left for a second animal clinic in Woburn, just 12 miles north of Boston. He was eager to buy his own clinic and start his own practice. (8)

He and Gina discovered a clinic in Duxbury, the second settlement of the Pilgrims and within sight of Alden House, which dated to 1653. Just 30 miles south of Boston, the village is perched on Duxbury Bay, which empties into Cape Cod Bay and the Atlantic Ocean. Hidden from the small road by saplings, the clinic was clean, but the second-floor living quarters needed substantial renovation. The shutters hung off the front of the house, and the yard was nothing but dirt and weeds.

So they went to work. They tore down walls, scraped off wallpaper and removed the window frames. They refurbished the hardwood floors, kitchen and bathrooms, replaced the doors, added a two-car garage and constructed a family room and glassed-in porch. They replaced the heating system and landscaped the front and back, spending so much money that Gina called it the "Money Pit." Ollie in particular enjoyed the family room because he had a penchant for watching television. His favorites were the "Rockford Files" and "The Life and Times of Grizzly Adams."

Every weekday morning, Bruce would be in the clinic by 6. He tended exclusively to small animals, mostly cats and dogs, along with rabbits, ferrets, mice, guinea pigs and hamsters. He hired a second veterinarian, an office manager, receptionist and a handful of technicians. He performed dentistry, orthopedic work and surgery on the neighbor's dogs and cats. The tenacity that allowed him to overcome the black Galaxie made him an ideal surgeon. He became a member of the American Animal Hospital Association, and every three years inspectors were impressed by his immaculate clinic.

He loved every aspect of caring for pets. One Easter a woman came in with a large dog that needed grooming, but all the groomers were booked. Not to worry, Bruce told her. On Sunday morning at 7:30, Bruce washed and combed the dog himself. (9) He loved veterinary work so much that he told Gina, "Sometimes I wish I had all the money in the world. You know what I would do with it? I would see animals for free and not have to charge for it." He refused to euthanize healthy animals, telling animal owners, "My business is healing." When an elderly woman's 100-pound Golden Retriever died in her house, she did not know what to do. So Bruce went out to her house and asked where she wanted to bury the dog. She pointed to the shade under a heavy tree. Bruce started digging, a job made more difficult because he kept striking the tree's thick roots. It was a humid mid-summer afternoon, and the work was taxing.

By the time he finished, his back ached. The distance between Michigan and Massachusetts helped dim the memory of the black Galaxie, but the sore back was a constant reminder. He had been in chronic back pain since the accident. He often brought it on simply by sitting in a chair or bending over. "It always hurts," he would tell friends.(10) He approached a surgeon in the 1980s, but decided there was nothing to do but live with the pain. Unlike Mike, Bruce dwelled neither on the past nor on his Birmingham friends. He had served as best man at Dick Lowrie's wedding, but after the move to Massachusetts they rarely talked. He wistfully acknowledged that he and Lowrie "sort of dropped the ball." Other friendships faded as well. In college, he briefly resumed dating Martha Jean Payton and went to her wedding in 1970, giving her a Waterford crystal ashtray as a present. Years later, Martha Jean's sister saw the ashtray and said, "I wouldn't mind having that." Martha Jean had not seen Bruce since Michigan State, but quickly replied, "No you won't."(11) Bruce occasionally saw Bill Saefkow in Florida where their parents had vacation homes. But Bruce and Bill drifted apart, too. Years later while on a business trip to Boston, Saefkow drove down to see Bruce and Gina. Bruce was glad Bill showed up. Bruce and Gina were getting their daughter Megan ready for school at the College of Charleston in South Carolina. But that would be the last time Saefkow would see his old friend.(12)

On fleeting occasions, he would think of Roddy. Every Christmas, Helen Henderson would send him a card, prompting him to say, "I would really like to see her."

The one person Bruce stayed close to was Mike Adair. When Mike helped organize a gathering of old Seaholm friends in 2003 at Crystal Lake near the Berridge cottage at Platte Lake, he persuaded Bruce to plan his Michigan vacation at the same time as the reunion. Sue Melcher was there. So were Sally Splane, Butch Fleming, Eddie Watkins and Nancy Ackerly. They played golf, took long boat rides, barbecued and drank beer. They snapped photos and laughed. "You guys are still kids," Sue Melcher's new husband told her. (13) When they did talk about the accident, they did so with the type of humor they aimed at Mike all his life. Nancy Ackerly teased him about having "such a hard head." But nobody kidded Bruce about that night in the Skylark. Bruce would never talk or joke about it. (14)

During that evening, Bruce asked Sue Melcher if she would join him for a walk to the nearby Berridge cottage. The stars glowed in the inky Michigan night. He asked about her kids, her new husband and if she was happy. She was, she assured him.

"I think about you," Bruce told her. "You're still a good friend of mine."

She understood. The crash, the deaths of Roddy, Peachie and Sandy would have been difficult for an adult to come to grips with. For teenagers, it had been virtually impossible. If Bruce coped with it from a distance, she thought, that was fine. Bruce and Mike were both sensitive and just as caring. They simply dealt with the horror of that evening in starkly different ways. (15)

Forty-one years after the accident in the winter of 2006, Bruce drove up to Vermont to see Mike and his first grandchild–Jessica's baby girl Jaya. Bruce and Mike lunched at Jessica's house, kept an eye on the baby girl, watched college basketball on television and ate a dinner prepared by Connie. Like Mike, Bruce decided he was lucky. "I've hardly had any wants in life. Gina, we've just been so happy."

On a clear evening in early August of 2005, they held a birthday party for Betty Adair. She was 90, and her six kids invited their families and a handful of close friends to Crystal Mountain. Corey Van Fleet was there. So was Mike's cousin Bob Adams. Betty's younger sister Dorothy flew in from Colorado. They sat at five round tables. There was fresh fish or steak for dinner and, as a joke, the kids included green beans–a reminder of the time that Betty snapped at Mike's daughter Elizabeth, then 6 years old, because she refused to eat them. Not used to being thwarted, Betty ordered Elizabeth to her room. But when Betty slammed the door, she inadvertently jammed the lock, forcing Mike to climb through a window and extricate Elizabeth from the room.

Betty stood without the help of her walker. That very morning when she woke up, she cracked, "Well, I made it." She joked that she talked too much and recalled the time in the 1960s when one of her sons tape-recorded her yelling at him. When she heard the tape, Betty said, "Geez, I sound like a witch," prompting Dr. Adair to dryly quip, "That's what I've had to listen to." Everybody at the party laughed. But she was moved by the memory of her husband. To the surprise of her daughters, Betty's voice broke.

They capped off the evening with a birthday cake. Nancy Adair snapped photos. On one wall of the dining room, the kids placed four large placards of family photos with the headline, "90 reasons why we love Betty." Each kid jotted down one of the 90 reasons. Mike wrote of Dr. Cooley repairing his aorta in Houston. "I remember it only took one elevator ride in the hospital for mom to tell our life story to strangers and to learn theirs," Mike wrote. "She has never been at a loss for words."

Mike's reference to the operation was part of a remarkable transformation. The physical reminders of the crash had always been there -- a stainless steel screen in his forehead, Dacron tube in his chest and a stainless steel wire in his right collarbone. Friends jokingly called Mike the $6 million man.

But he had avoided talking about the black Galaxie. Now, as he approached age 58, that was changing. Mike telephoned Alex Grether, the boy who held him still in the Skylark until the ambulances arrived. He telephoned John Schaeffer, whose father had tried so desperately to keep Roddy, Peachie and Sandy alive. He called Janice Poplack, the only person he could confide in during those months after the wreck. He went to Manistee to see Corey Van Fleet, who lived with his wife in a rustic home on a small lake. He drove to Harbor Springs to see Susie Martin's parents, and they laughed about the time he and Bruce tried to give them a pet monkey. He telephoned Sandy Christman's younger sister Donna. He talked by phone with Dr. Bob Pool, one of the surgeons who pumped blood into him that night in the operating room at Beaumont. He visited Helen Henderson at the senior center she lived at in Rochester, presenting her with flowers and chatting with Helen and Nancy Henderson.

A few days later, Helen sent an appreciative note. "What a great time we had talking about so many different mutual interests," Helen wrote. "You were so kind to take the time to come out and see Nancy and me. Your lovely bouquet of flowers is much appreciated. Such a beautiful blend of yellows and deep pink. Glad you brought the wonderful picture of your family. Love to you and your family, Helen Henderson."

TWELVE

"Sunset and Evening Star"

Normally, the carillons' 46 bells chimed out cheery music, particularly for the summer concerts that drew packed crowds to the manicured green lawns. But on this Saturday afternoon in January of 1965, they were silent. It was two weeks after Roddy Henderson, Peachie Barnum and Sandy Christman died and the families asked for a special service for their Seaholm friends who had not been able to attend the services held on school days. They selected Christ Church Cranbrook, an ornamental sandstone structure nestled in Bloomfield Hills, an area of rolling knolls, stately pines and narrow winding roads. The church had a massive stained-glass window honoring famous women, including Susan B. Anthony, Emily Dickinson and Harriet Beecher Stowe. Scores of mourners, young and old, tramped through the heavy snow to the church. The service was expanded to include Mike Drothler. The church bulletin misspelled Roddy's first name, the same old mistake of adding the "d" to Roger. The service opened with a hymn and a reading from Psalms 46. The mourners sang a second hymn and recited the Lord's Prayer. Then a third hymn.

Dr. G. Ernest Thomas, the minister at the First Methodist Church in Birmingham, stood before the crowd: "Only a few days ago, these colleagues of ours, these fellow-students – we saw them, talked with them, we enjoyed our recreation and social life with them. Now in the suddenness of a single moment, life is over. And we're brought face-to-face with what the writer of Proverbs was talking of so many years ago. 'Thou knowest not what a day may bring forth.' "

Dr. Thomas tried to find some meaning for the mourners in what seemed an utterly senseless tragedy. The Birmingham police chief had said that Roddy and his friends had simply been "in the wrong place, at the wrong time." But Dr. Thomas saw something different: It wasn't fate or bad luck that Roddy and his friends happened to be driving up Maple the night of January 16. Though Dr. Thomas never mentioned Mike Drothler, his speeding black Galaxie, the curve in the road that he missed, the minister's meaning was clear: Break the laws of nature and tragedy occurs. "The law of gravity is basic in the life of the universe," Dr. Thomas said. "When a child steps too close to a precipice, he falls over and perishes. When an airplane engine fails to function, then the plane can no longer maintain its height and it crashes . . . The occasion that brings us together is a reminder that one cannot break the laws that have to do with gravity and have to do with the moral life of man, and yet prosper in God's world."

He concluded by reading "Crossing the Bar," which Alfred Lord Tennyson penned at age 81 in anticipation of his own death. What Dr. Thomas did not know was that it was the same poem Roddy so laboriously copied for his class assignment a few years earlier and which so annoyed his junior high teacher. "Take the greatest mind of the last century, towering over any intellect of his day," Dr. Thomas said. "Hear him as he speaks again to you on an afternoon like this, the words that came from his pen:

"Sunset and evening star,
And one clear call for me!
And may there be no moaning of the bar,
When I put out to sea,

But such a tide as moving seems asleep,
Too full for sound and foam,
When that which drew from out the boundless deep
Turns again home.

Twilight and evening bell,
And after that the dark!
And may there be no sadness of farewell,
When I embark;

For tho' from out our bourne of Time and Place
The flood may bear me far,

I hope to see my Pilot face to face
When I have crost the bar." (1)

Nobody seemed to forget during the next four decades, none could understand. "You're talking to people in their mid-50s and how vividly they remember one week of their lives," one of Roddy's Seaholm teammates said in 2005.(2) Every January 16, Alex Grether thinks about holding Mike Adair still in the Skylark's wreckage. Mark Morden tells people he wished he had driven that night—as he had done so often with Roddy, Bruce and Mike. He would have taken Oak Street instead of Maple. But he had a date that night and could not join his best friends. Years after the crash, one close friend dreamt of sitting at a table with Roddy, Peachie and Sandy. "What's it like to be dead?" she asked them. The three kids replied, "We can't give you any more information." Another friend recalled a story that one of the mothers forgot to tell the kids, "Have a good time," as they left that night. She never forgot to say that sentence any time her own kids left the house. As she rummaged through an old jewelry box in 2008, Betsy Brenton found the silver charm that Sandy Christman brought back from Mexico and gave her just before her death. She showed the charm to her daughter and two granddaughters.

"A day doesn't go by where I don't think of Peachie and those kids," said Patty Barnum. Nancy Henderson said it took years to "come to terms with having had a wonderful childhood that ended way too abruptly." As Jim Henderson, always stoic and imperturbable, spoke of Roddy years later, he suddenly burst into uncontrollable sobs. "We had just become so close," he said of his younger brother. Shortly after turning 60, Jim wrote, "We still mourn the brevity of the lives of Peachie, Sandy and Roddy." Krisa Barnum often pleaded with her husband to drive slower than the speed limit. "You don't know what it's like to lose someone," she would tell him.

On a Sunday in January of 2005, Mike Adair saw an old high school friend in a Birmingham church and quietly said, "Forty years ago today."(3) During the early summer of 2005, Bruce Berridge's old girlfriend Martha Jean Payton joined four other women friends for a week of hiking and Bible study at Pictured Rocks off Lake Superior in the Upper Peninsula. On the last night following a grueling afternoon of hiking, they showered, changed into pajamas and lounged about their rented cabin. When one woman asked if they had ever been angry with God, Martha Jean found herself talking about the accident. She had been so angry. How could God have allowed this to happen? The accident had shaken her faith; it took her years to regain her religious beliefs.

Jay Hengelmann, who had nearly died in 1961 when Mike Drothler drove his 1955 Chevy into a telephone pole near Lake Park, moved to Arizona where he became a juvenile probation officer. He often encountered kids who had been picked up while drinking beer in their cars. Hengelmann would ritually tell them, "You don't know how lucky you are to get pulled over. Let me tell you what happened to a friend of mine." Then he would recount the night that Mike Drothler rammed his black Galaxie into the burgundy Skylark. When Roy Monsour, a friend of Mike Drothler's, found out in 2008 that Fred and Dottie Drothler apologized in person to the Barnums, Hendersons and Christmans, his voice broke with emotion. "That doesn't surprise me at all," he said. "Fred was a salt of the earth type guy. He played by the rules all the time."

In the first year after Roddy's death, Anne Le Fevre constantly dreamed about him, including one where he kissed her in algebra class. "I think about him constantly," she wrote Helen Henderson one year after the crash. She dwelled on the "wonderful memories" of Roddy and when she did, she found herself breaking out in her trademark "Roddy smile." After graduation from college and marriage, she moved to upstate New York, where she and Helen chatted by telephone, exchanged Christmas cards and made a point of writing each other on Roddy's birthday. Every January 16, Anne scribbled a note to Helen saying, "I wanted you to know that I remembered." (4)

Helen Henderson kept collecting memories of Roddy. In the late 1970s, Sue Melcher and Anne Le Fevre arranged to give Helen the plaque honoring Roddy that Seaholm officials had placed near the school pool. Thirty years after the accident, Helen appeared before the Oakland County chapter of Mothers Against Drunk Driving. She spoke of the Hendersons, Barnums and Christmans enduring the "endless grief over Roddy's and the girls' deaths." She pointed out that Nancy and Roddy had been "especially close, and Nancy suffered probably more than any of us. A young person does not receive the support that adults usually do—children and teens tend not to know what to say or do to help a friend who has had such a loss." She said that she and Ed suffered the loss "that every parent dreads" when their 16-year-olds begin to drive. "There is no replacing a precious son—an outstanding young person whose bright future was obliterated by one reckless drunk driver." When she moved into an apartment for senior citizens in 2004, she placed three framed black-and-white photographs of Jim, Roddy and Nancy on a table. They were photos taken as teenagers, when Roddy was alive and life was so joyful.

With typical gusto in 2006, Mike threw himself into helping organize the 40th re-union of his high school class. He served on a committee of 1966 graduates that met at night to plan the event, although he joked he did little more than show up and eat a free dinner. They selected a Saturday evening in June and arranged to hold the re-union at the Community House uptown. Mike contacted old classmates, invited Nancy Henderson as a special guest, and pleaded with Bruce Berridge to fly from Boston to Michigan for the event. But Bruce said he could not make it; someone, he explained, had to be at the veterinary clinic that weekend.

On the Friday evening before the re-union, John Allman, Roddy's old buddy, threw a party at his colonial home on Lake Park in Birmingham. Mike spent the afternoon at the house, setting up folding tables, covering them with cloths and devising a nostalgic menu that included a keg of beer, Coney dogs and 80 hamburgers from the Hunter House in Birmingham–a Seaholm staple in 1965. Hunter House hamburgers were notorious for their thick buns, pickles, mustard, onions and tiny slivers of beef. Nearly 60 people gathered around Allman's sparkling pool on this clear and cool Michigan summer evening. Those who realized the house was just down the street from Henderson's Light did not saying anything.

Five Seaholm graduates from the 1960s–including Roddy's old friend Steve Matthews–had formed a band of aging baby boomers, called themselves Dr. Fred and blared away on guitars, organ and drums. Their specialties were "I Saw Her Standing There" by the Beatles, "We Gotta To Get Out Of This Place," by the Animals and Van Morrison's "Brown-Eyed Girl." The guests danced for hours. Nancy Henderson, who was invited to the party, thought the evening reminded her of a Jimmy Buffet concert with guys wearing Hawaiian shirts and khaki shorts. She was surprised when first John Allman, and then Steve Matthews, recognized her and hugged her. (5)

The next evening at the Community House, nearly 150 members of the class of 1966 gathered for drinks and dinner. Mike hugged the friends he had been so determined to stay in touch with. Everybody laughed at a high school photograph of Mike Adair, Bruce Berridge and Mark Morden sitting on a couch and casually flipping their middle fingers, an act of teenage defiance.

But for Mike, something was not quite right. He missed his oldest and closest friend. Grasping his cell phone, Mike dialed Bruce Berridge's number in Massachusetts and left a voice message. A short while later, Mike's cell phone beeped. It was Bruce.

When he saw Nancy Henderson walk in, Mike was happy. Roddy's old friends surrounded her. One woman recalled Roddy singing "Matilda" at Quarton and how she instantly fell for him. One classmate remembered Roddy as "Mr. Cool," as the man told Nancy–wearing a sport coat without lapels, a pencil-thin tie and neatly creased slacks. If Roddy were here this evening, he would have walked in with a woman on each arm, the man said. Nancy laughed with Mike Adair, Butch Fleming, John Allman and Mark Morden–still Roddy's best friends after 40 years. She produced a camera and

184

clicked away. She wanted to remember everyone who still thought about Roddy.

For Nancy, it was an evening of discovery. For years, she assumed that nobody really remembered her talented older brother. She had felt so solitary in her grief. Now on this night, surrounded by people who knew and loved Roddy and Peachie and Sandy, she realized she was wrong. They had been just as deeply affected by their deaths as she had been. I'm not alone with that, she thought, and never will be again.

Jim Henderson did not write poems as his sister did or save mementos like his mother. He immersed himself in Business News, adding new magazines and presiding over a prosperous expansion. But as his three sons and daughter grew up, he became compulsive about their being home on time from every date or outing. If they were even a few minutes late, he would be filled with anxiety about an accident. "All my life, I was waiting for that call," he said years later. Jim worried so much that his wife finally admonished the kids about being home on time. "You've got to stop doing this," she told them. "You can't put your dad through this."(6)

Finally, the call came: His daughter Breanna, whom they called Bree, had been in an accident in Canada, not far from the Blue Water Bridge that links Sarnia to Port Huron. Her boyfriend, who had not been drinking, lost control of the family SUV, and it flipped over, tossing Bree from the car. She fractured her pelvis and suffered a traumatic brain injury. A friend arranged to have Bree flown by helicopter to the advanced medical center at the University of Michigan. For nearly four weeks, Jim and his wife Robin made certain somebody from the family was with Bree 24 hours a day. After much physical therapy and rehabilitation, she completely recovered and by the spring of 2005 earned a master's degree at Wayne State in physical therapy.

On a Sunday afternoon 40 years after his brother's death, Jim Henderson thumbed through some old family albums he had not seen in years. He found a photo of the two brothers standing together, no more than ages 6 and 3. There was another photograph of the two taken a couple of years later. And finally, a photo of Roddy snapped in the final year of his life. Jim framed the photos and placed them on a shelf in his study.

You can find Roddy in the Greenwood Cemetery, near Quarton Lake where he and his friends ice skated in winter and not far from Henderson's Light. His grave lies at the front of the Henderson plot, resting on a high bluff that overlooks a small fieldstone bridge spanning the Rouge River. Roddy's father and grandmother are just a few feet away. A spot has been reserved for Helen. Large evergreens shade Roddy's headstone, which simply says, "Roger Leeman Henderson, September 29, 1948 –January 16, 1965."

Eddie Watkins is a regular visitor, in part because his parents are buried in the same cemetery. On a frigid December day in 2005, he flew in from his San Diego home for a family re-union. He and a brother and sister stopped at Greenwood, first standing over the graves of their parents and then trudging through the heavy snow to Roddy's. Daylight was fading on this grim, cloudy afternoon, so typical for Detroit in December. It should never have happened, Watkins kept thinking. Roddy had been so sick that day, he should have been home applying Vicks to his chest rather than out having pizza with friends. But Roddy, he thought, loved life too much to waste a Saturday night.

Butch Fleming, who moved to Indiana as an adult, often returns to stand silently before Roddy's grave and ask himself over and over the question Reverend Thomas tried to answer and Jack Barnum never could. Why? It was so senseless. Roddy had it all. Good looks, athletic ability, clever mind. Years later, Fleming returned to Birmingham to attend the funeral of a friend's mother. But he set aside time to see his old friend's grave. He drove to the cemetery's far end, parked his car and walked toward the northwest corner. Butch was now in his late 50s, as Roddy should have been.

"OK, Roddy, I still don't understand," Butch said to himself.

Nancy Henderson often stopped by, sitting by herself or walking down to the river to watch the ducks and muskrats. She almost never cried, but found the area comforting, wondering how her life would have been different had Roddy lived. There was a plot of ground that already had been set aside for her as well.

A week after the reunion, Nancy visited Roddy's grave. She noticed that soot and dirt had blackened the headstones for Roddy, her father and grandmother over the years. It was getting harder to read the names, she thought. At Roddy's class reunion, Nancy had been struck by the number of people who still visited his grave. If so many people are coming out here, Nancy thought, then perhaps she should clean the headstones. The next day, she returned with a pail, some Simple Green and a scrub brush.

Sandy and Peachie are several miles away in the White Chapel Cemetery, at the corner of Long Lake and Crooks roads in Troy. Sandy's ashes rest in a small bronze urn with a glass front on the third floor of the chapel. It reads, "Sandra Helene Christman, 1947-1965." Peachie is outside the chapel in the cemetery, within sight of a statute of St. Francis of Assisi. The grave marker, heavily covered by thick grass, is difficult to find. "Barbara J. Barnum, beloved daughter and sister, 1948 1965."

A few days after the memorial service for Jack and Betty in 1986, the Barnum sisters drove back to White Chapel and took two canisters from their trunk. One contained the torpedo bomber's ashes, the other Betty's. Just as they began to sprinkle the ashes over Peachie's grave marker, a huge gust of wind scattered them about. The sisters couldn't decide whether to laugh or cry. (7)

The traffic light at the corner of Lake Park and Maple served as the visible reminder to everyone. Sue Melcher would drive past Henderson's Light every day and think of Roddy and Peachie and Sandy. Donna Bell said she has "never driven by there without thinking of those three."

For others, Henderson's Light generated too much anguish. Dr. Adair assiduously avoided that corner, telling Betty, "I just can't drive by that place."(8) But his son Mike did go back. On a Saturday night not long ago, he was inside the Silverdome near Pontiac, running a concession stand to help raise money for his daughter Elizabeth's chool marching band. By the time he closed the stand and turned his car south on Woodward Avenue, it was dark. With his wife Connie out of town, there was no rush to get home, so he impulsively made a little detour. Just before he reached the heart of uptown Birmingham, he turned right on Oak Street, the road that Mark Morden said he would have taken that night in 1965. He drove past the main gate of the Greenwood Cemetery and thought of Roddy and the grave he visited so often. Then left on Lake Park and into the neighborhood he knew so well–where Roddy played his Beach Boys' albums, Bruce fired his BB gun at wasps' nests, Peachie hosted her sleepovers, Sandy drove her go-cart and Mike dreamed of becoming a doctor. He passed Quarton Lake on the left before reaching Henderson's Light. He stopped the car. It was 10:30 on this Saturday evening of January 16, 2004–exactly 39 years after Mike Drothler's black Galaxie smashed into Roddy's Skylark and changed so many lives. It was quiet; not a car in sight, unlike that night in 1965 with its popping explosion, shattered cars and screeching sirens. All he knew about that night was what others told him. He waited a few seconds before continuing on Maple into uptown Birmingham and the turn on Woodward that would take him home.

EPILOGUE

In the summer of 2008, Bruce Berridge kept a longstanding promise he had made to himself and visited Helen Henderson. On a Friday morning, he, Mike and Connie met Nancy Henderson in the lobby of the senior center where Helen lived. When he saw Nancy, Bruce hugged her and said, "Wow, it's probably been 35 years." Except for his gray hair, Nancy thought Bruce looked exactly the same as he did when she knew him as a kid in Birmingham–and just like his dad.

They went up to the third floor where Helen was waiting. Bruce gave her a big hug and Helen smiled. For the next hour they talked of better times; of the night Bruce and Roddy tossed cherry bombs in neighborhood mailboxes, of the Halloween evening when the three boys stole the next-door neighbor's pumpkin, and of those summer afternoons when Roddy, Bruce and Mike raced their bikes along the sloping walls of the pond at Cranbrook. Helen peppered Mike and Bruce with questions about their kids and Mike showed photos of his grandchildren.

Bruce, Mike, Nancy and Connie then went to a nearby restaurant where they relaxed at a table on the outdoor patio. It was a windy, but warm afternoon. Bruce and Mike recalled the night at the pizza parlor where Mike kept tossing pizza crust across the table for Bruce to eat. After the crash, Mike told them, he "couldn't eat pizza for a long time and I couldn't figure out why."

It was Mike's 60th birthday. He and Bruce had tickets to the Tigers' game that night in Comerica Park.

The people at the table were at the center of a four-year effort on my part to piece together this accident. When I first began researching "Henderson's Light" in December of 2004, I planned to focus on Mike Adair and Bruce Berridge and follow their lives to the present day. But I quickly realized that I could not separate Mike and Bruce from the friends and relatives of Roddy, Peachie, and Sandy Christman. It became obvious that this crash, like virtually all car crashes involving alcohol, left permanent scars on friends and families that time did not heal. Some people broke down and wept in front of me as they described the crash. Others, such as Peachie's close friend Suzanne Witbeck, simply could not bear discussing it. I made repeated efforts to contact Sandy Christman's sister Donna by letter and telephone, but she chose not to be interviewed for this book. I have respected her decision.

But others agreed to talk and without their help this book could never have been written. From the time Mike Adair first responded in January of 2005 to an e-mail I sent his sister, I have interviewed more than 125 people. Many consented to numerous interviews, and some read the manuscript for accuracy and suggested revisions.

I am particularly grateful to Nancy Henderson, Jim Henderson, Helen Henderson, Mike Adair, Bruce Berridge, Patty Barnum Moorhead, Krisa Barnum, Jacquey Barnum Piallat and Robert Drothler. Nancy Henderson made available all the diaries she faithfully recorded for four decades, allowing me to reconstruct in painstaking detail the everyday life of the Henderson family. During interviews at her home in suburban Detroit, she showed me the huge collection of mementos her mother Helen kept. She persuaded me that any story of the crash had to include the impact it had on all the families. She read through every draft of the manuscript and suggested changes. In a surprise to me, Helen asked to see me in person and provided me with humorous and touching recollections of Roddy. Jim Henderson, the first member of his family to talk with me, agreed to a lengthy interview in his home in Bloomfield Hills, and then read the manuscript.

Patty Barnum Moorhead not only agreed to an interview in her home in suburban Phoenix, but also provided me with personal letters written by her mother Betty and her sister Peachie. She made available a huge scrapbook of Jack Barnum's letters during World War II, which were invaluable in reconstructing the life of this remarkable man. I traveled to South Carolina to interview Krisa Barnum and conducted repeated interviews by telephone with Jacquey Barnum Piallat.

Mike Adair spent countless hours in person and by telephone describing the aftermath of the accident and the surgeries he endured. He is one of the warmest and funniest people I have ever known. When I first traveled to Birmingham in April of 2005, he invited me to his house for dinner. His brothers and sisters offered dramatic details of Mike's recovery from the crash. His wife Connie provided crucial information about Mike's fifth surgery and carefully read the final manuscript. His mother Betty, a reporter's dream because she is so easy to talk with, made available legal documents, personal letters and medical bills. Nancy Adair showed me the diary she kept in 1965, which, like Nancy Henderson's diary, allowed me to recreate the days after the crash. Mike suggested I contact his first wife, Sue Watkins Adair, and she agreed to an interview that was insightful and helpful. Mike then invited me to attend Betty's 90th birthday party at Crystal Lake where I met his entire family.

By contrast to Mike Adair, Bruce Berridge was more reluctant to talk. When I flew to Massachusetts to interview him in January of 2006, it was clear he dreaded the thought of discussing the accident. He had done his best to put that night behind him. But he is one of the nicest people anyone could hope to meet and he spent hours in his home in Duxbury talking about Mike, Roddy, Peachie, Sandy and his own remarkable recovery. Bruce's brother Jim provided invaluable help during repeated phone interviews and a lengthy interview at the family cottage at Platte Lake, where he and Bruce spent their summers as kids.

Corey Van Fleet, in a number of telephone interviews and an interview at his home near Traverse City, described in detail the great Seaholm swimming teams and that horrifying night when he identified Roddy in the emergency room. Van Fleet, Ted Blakeslee, Chuck Geggie, Dave Zimmer, and Steve Zimmer helped me recreate the era when Seaholm dominated Michigan swimming.

The Birmingham police department searched through its files but could not locate the accident record. But Herb Duncan and Harold Jones, the police officers who responded to the accident, provided with me with their recollections. Tom Raupp, whose father was driving the car behind Roddy's Skylark, vividly recalled the moment before impact. Bob Lyndall, Jim McGowan, Tom Lawton, John B.

191

Schaeffer, Alex Grether, Allan Mee, John Matthews, and Bill Balsley were eyewitnesses to the crash scene, with Grether retelling how he cradled Mike Adair to keep him from moving. Robert Pool, one of the physicians in the operating room that night at Beaumont Hospital, provided details of how surgeons saved Mike's life, while Dr. Denton Cooley provided details of Mike Adair's operation in Houston.

Robert Drothler, Mike's younger brother, spent several hours in telephone interviews talking about his brother and parents. He suggested the names of Mike's classmates from Brentwood who might help. Jay Hengelmann, who survived Mike Drothler's first crash in 1961, and his mother Kay gave me their recollections of Mike and his parents. I am also grateful for the help provided by Liz Hemlinger Parise, Roy Monsour, Nick Monsour, Wesley Sharrer, Marjorie Ann Enock Anderson, B.J. Hengelmann, known in 1961 as Betty Jo, Larry Ducharme, Gary Moorhead and Bob Zane.

I deeply appreciated how many Seaholm graduates took the time to find their old school yearbooks and read me the notes their friends had scribbled. In particular, I want to thank Sally Splane McWilliams, Nancy Ackerly Barton, Anne Le Fevre Haller, Susan Banes Loss, Susan Weil Miller, Nancy Yaryan Skatberg, Ellen Tower Bayless, Judy Frederick, and Martha Hamilton Cleamons. Susan Melcher Pomroy, who works at Seaholm, suggested people to contact as well as her recollections of Peachie, Bruce, Mike, Roddy and Sandy. Susan Martin Hyde dug through old boxes at her parents' home to send me photos of Mike and Bruce recovering from the accident.

Donna Bell Zimmer showed me old newspaper clippings of the crash and her old yearbooks during an interview at her home. She helped me contact other members of the Seaholm class of 1966. She joined Mike Adair, Sue Pomroy and Sally Splane McWilliams in inviting me to their class re-union in June of 2006. In addition, I want to thank the following people who generously gave their time to provide recollections of the crash: Bob Adams, Gina Berridge, John Allman, Ed Watkins, Vicki Hogan, Bill Keough, Betty Haugh Crowder, Gary Witbeck, Greg Witbeck, Mark Morden, Paul Fleming,

Steve Matthews, Michael Keener, Robert Martin, Marian Martin, Dick Lowrie, Bob Poplack, Gwen Straight, Dick Straight, Bill Crandell, Dave Nelson, Larry Ross, Janice Poplack, Jack Payton, Tony Menkel, Carla Jolly Cleary, Bill Bowering, Graham Bullock, Nancy Wawak Evangelista, Martha Jean Payton Smith, Cheryl Kravis Greenberg, Donna Richardson Buchanan, Peggy Boyle Goldberg, Sally Shepherd, Bill Canning, Linda Canning King, Meredith Martin Cronyn, Katherine Moorhead, Juanita Cooper, Josie Campbell Rock, Cynthia Calderwood, Jan Weidner Moreas, Carol Wollenberg Wedge, Patricia Pitcher Parks, Betsy Brenton Conant, Margie Rainey, Linda Peitz, Burke Lewis, Tim Williams, Susan Berry, Lesley Swatman Bennett, Linda Stubbs Pierce, Bill Saefkow, Susan Saefkow Brown, Dave Seed, Dorothy Clemens, Jim Farr, Frank Roberts, Charles Grenadier, Judy Kieppe Nelson, Karen Kieppe Boyd, Nancy Jo Hutchins, Barbara Heinz, Catryn John Loos, Andrea Holcomb Gardner, and Deborah Harter Williams.

The Birmingham *Eccentric* and Seaholm, Barnum and Derby school yearbooks are on file at the Birmingham Public Library. The Library of Congress in Washington offered the files of the *Detroit Free Press* and *Detroit News*, while the Brentwood Public Library in suburban Pittsburgh had the Brentwood High yearbooks. The principal at Quarton Elementary School gave me a tour of the school, including the elevated stage where so many years ago, a young Roddy delighted his friends by singing *Matilda*.

I also appreciated Katherine Albrecht of the Bloomfield Hills law firm of Beier, Howlett for helping me locate the lawsuit filed by the Adairs and Berridges against the Drothler family. I also want to thank my agent, Diane Nine, who believed in this project, and most importantly, my wife, Saundra Torry of *USA Today*, who spent so much time editing the manuscript

NOTES

CHAPTER ONE

"Mr. Cool"

1. Interview with Corey Van Fleet.
2. Teammates Bruce Berridge, Tom Lawton and Ed Watkins provided a good description of Roddy's lax work habits.
3. Interview with Corey Van Fleet.
4. The Detroit Free Press, January 18, 1965.
5. His name is spelled Roger on his birth certificate.
6. Interview with Helen Henderson.
7. Interviews with Nancy Henderson and Bruce Berridge.
8. Interview with Dave Nelson.
9. Interviews with Jim Henderson and Helen Henderson.
10. There are two slightly different versions of Roddy's poem. One was published in 1966 by the Seaholm student newspaper. But he also typed out the original for his English class at Seaholm in February 1964. I have chosen to use the second, which includes his hand-written corrections.
11. Roddy's spiral notebook includes the teacher's comments.
12. Mike Adair recounted the conversation with Roddy and Ed Watkins.
13. Anne Le Fevre Haller said that Roddy wasn't sure if he wanted to sing the solo.
14. Interview with Nancy Henderson.
15. Nancy Henderson's diary, February 9, 1964.
16. Interview with Ted Blakeslee.
17. Interviews with Nancy Henderson, Steve Matthews, Bill Keough and Tom Lawton.
18. Letter from Anne Le Fevre to Helen Henderson, January 19, 1966.
19. Letter from Anne Le Fevre to Helen Henderson, May 5, 1965.
20. Anne Le Fevre Haller's 1963 Barnum yearbook.

21. Roddy typed the sonnet on the same typewriter he used a month later for his swimming poem in English class. Unlike the swimming poem, which he signed 'Roddy," he signed the sonnet "Roger." There is no indication that it was a class assignment. Nor is there any way of knowing that he ever showed it to anyone. Anne Le Fevre Haller does not recall ever receiving the sonnet. Nancy Henderson discovered the sonnet in a file kept by her grandmother, Jesse Leeman Henderson, who was a poet.
22. A note Roddy scribbled in Susan Weil Miller's 1964 Seaholm yearbook.
23. Letter from Suzanne Pratt to Helen Henderson, March 4, 1965.
24. Interview with Ted Blakeslee.
25. Interview with Ted Blakeslee.
26. Interview with Chuck Geggie.
27. Interview with Tom Lawton.
28. The Detroit News, February 15, 1964.
29. Nancy Henderson's diary, March 29, 1964.
30. Nancy Henderson's diary entries from June 21-24, 1964 provide the details of the Hidden Valley trip.
31. Interviews with Steve Matthews, Nancy Henderson and Linda Stubbs Pierce.
32. The Oakland Hills club bulletin, October 1964. Nancy Henderson won an award for the best 13-year-old girl swimmer.
33. Interview with Nancy Henderson.
34. Interview with Jim Henderson.
35. Nancy Henderson's diary entries for December 24-28, 1964.

CHAPTER TWO

"The Aviator's daughter"

1. Detroit Free Press, January 18, 1965.
2. Interview with Chuck Geggie.
3. Interview with Corey Van Fleet.

4. Interview with Betsy Brenton Conant.
5. Interview with Carol Wollenberg Wedge.
6. Interview with Krisa Barnum.
7. Interviews with Betsy Brenton Conant, Nancy Yaryan Skatberg and Susan Banes Loss.
8. Interviews with Jacquey Barnum Piallat and Patty Barnum Moorhead.
9. Interview with Patty Barnum Moorhead.
10. Birmingham Eccentric, July 20, 1967.
11. Interview with Patty Barnum Moorhead.
12. Interview with Krisa Barnum.
13. Interview with Linda Peitz Kemp.
14. Interview with Susan Banes Loss.
15. Interview with Susan Banes Loss.
16. Peachie scribbled the note in Sally Splane McWilliams' Derby yearbook.
17. Interviews with Josie Campbell Rock, Betsy Brenton Conant and Cindy Calderwood.
18. Interview with Linda Canning King.
19. Interview with Gary Moorhead.
20. Letter from Jack Barnum to his father, February 9, 1941.
21. Letters from Jack Barnum to his father, December 30, 1940, and February 23, 1941.
22. Torpedo 8, by Ira Wolfert.
23. Letter of commendation by Jack Barnum's commanding officer, August 27, 1942.
24. Jack described the flight to the Saratoga to a reporter from the Youngstown Vindicator, January 1, 1943.
25. Jack received separate letters from Admiral Chester Nimitz and Secretary of the Navy Frank Knox for his attack during the battle of the Eastern Solomons on August 24, 1942. The five Avengers were joined by two Dauntless dive bombers and they reported spotting four Japanese heavy cruisers, six light cruisers and six destroyers toward dusk. The Japanese fleet of 34 ships had been divided into four separate squadrons and the task force

that comes closest to matching the one Jack attacked was commanded by Admiral Nobutake Kondo, comprised of the modern heavy cruisers Atago, Maya, Haguro, Myoko and Takao – one light cruiser, six destroyers and the 12,000-ton seaplane carrier Chitose, whose superstructure would have resembled a cruiser to any aviator. None of the Japanese ships reported being struck by torpedoes, but the dive bombers scored two hits on the Chitose, putting her out of action for two months.

26. Youngstown Vindicator, January 1, 1943.
27. Interview Eddie Watkins.
28. Interview with Ellen Tower Bayless.
29. Interview with Bill Keough.
30. Interviews with Susan Banes Loss and Susan Weil Miller.
31. Interview with Betsy Brenton Conant.
32. Interview with Helen Henderson.
33. Interview with Anne Le Fevre Haller.
34. Interview with Betsy Brenton Conant.
35. Interview with Patricia Pitcher Parks.

CHAPTER THREE

"The Jokester"

1. Helen Henderson's scoreboard was among the papers she saved.
2. Detroit Free Press, January 18, 1965.
3. Interview with Ted Blakeslee.
4. Detroit Free Press, January 18, 1965.
5. Interview with Jim Henderson.
6. Interview with Mark Morden.
7. Nancy Henderson's diary, October 19, 1964.
8. Notes scribbled by friends in Mike Adair's eighth and ninth-grade Barnum yearbooks.
9. A note by Bruce Berridge in Mike Adair's eighth-grade yearbook in 1962.

10. Ibid.
11. Mike Adair wrote the note in Ellen Tower Bayless' yearbook.
12. Interview with Sally Splane McWilliams.
13. Interview with Janice Poplack.
14. A note by Nancy Wawak Evangelista in Mike Adair's ninth-grade yearbook.
15. Interview with Bill Canning.
16. Bruce Berridge referred to Mike's crooked nose in the 1962 yearbook note.
17. Interview with Mike Adair.
18. Interview with Dick Lowrie.
19. Barnum swim coach Richard Moran made that prediction in Mike's ninth-grade yearbook.
20. A note by Burke Lewis in Mike's ninth-grade yearbook.
21. Interview with Betty Adair.
22. Interviews with Mike Adair and Nancy Adair.
23. Interview with Nancy Adair.
24. Nancy Adair's diary, August 23, 1964.
25. Interview with Nancy Adair.
26. Nancy Adair's diary, September 6, 1964.
27. Nancy Adair provides details of the vacation in her diary entries from August 22-31, 1964.

CHAPTER FOUR

"Your friend always, Bruce Berridge"

1. Interviews with Janice Poplack, Nancy Ackerly Barton and Nancy Wawak Evangelista.
2. Interview with Linda Stubbs Pierce.
3. Interview with Martha Jean Payton Smith.
4. A note Bruce scribbled in Mike Adair's eighth-grade yearbook.
5. Interview with Donna Bell Zimmer.
6. Interview with Jim Berridge.

7. Interview with Bill Saefkow.
8. Interviews with Bruce Berridge and Jim Berridge.
9. Interview with Bruce Berridge.
10. Interview with Bill Saefkow.
11. Interviews with Bruce Berridge and Jim Berridge.
12. Interviews with Bruce Berridge and Mike Adair.
13. Interviews with Bruce Berridge and Jim Berridge.
14. Interview with Bruce Berridge.
15. Interview with Bruce Berridge.
16. Interview with Mike Adair.
17. Interviews with Mike Adair and Eddie Watkins.
18. Roddy wrote the note in the spring of 1964 in the 10th-grade yearbook of Judy Frederick. Bruce wrote his note to Frederick in 1962 in her Barnum Junior High yearbook.
19. Interview with Bill Saefkow.
20. Interview with Jim Berridge.
21. Interview with Bruce Berridge.
22. Interview with Bill Saefkow.
23. Interview with Bill Saefkow.

CHAPTER FIVE

"At home in a car"

1. Interview with Betsy Brenton Conant.
2. Interview with Donna Bell Zimmer.
3. Interviews with Donna Bell Zimmer and Lesley Swatman Bennett.
4. Interview with Donna Bell Zimmer.
5. Interview with Linda Stubbs Pierce.
6. The Detroit News, January 18, 1965.
7. Interview with Cindy Calderwood.
8. Martha Hamilton Cleamons' 1961 Derby yearbook.
9. The Detroit Free Press, January 19, 1965.

10. Nancy Yaryan Skadberg's 1962 and 1963 Derby yearbooks.
11. Detroit Free Press, January 18, 1965.
12. Interview with Frank Roberts.
13. Interview with Carla Jolly Cleary.
14. Interview with Lesley Swatman Bennett.
15. Interview with Frank Roberts.
16. Interview with Peggy Boyle.
17. Brentwood High School yearbook, 1960.
18. Interviews with Nick Monsour and Roy Monsour and the 1960 Brentwood High yearbook.
19. Interview with Liz Hemlinger Parise.
20. Interview with Bob Zane.
21. Interview with Robert Drothler.
22. Interview with Robert Drothler.
23. Fred Drothler supplied a list of his assets and liabilities to Dean Beier, an attorney in Pontiac who represented the Adairs and Berridges after the accident. Betty Adair kept copies of those records.
24. Interview with Robert Drothler.
25. Interview with Liz Hemlinger Parise.
26. Interviews with Larry Ducharme, Jay Hengelmann and B.J. Hengelmann, and the Birmingham Eccentric, January 21, 1965.
27. Interviews with Jay Hengelmann and Kay Hengelmann.
28. Birmingham Eccentric, January 21, 1965.
29. Bob Zane said his mother saw Mike Drothler late in the afternoon of the 1965 accident. Police discovered the two cases of beer and six steaks in the wreckage of the Galaxie, according to the Birmingham Eccentric, January 21, 1965.
30. Birmingham Eccentric, January 21, 1965.

CHAPTER SIX

"We've got a bunch of kids in this car."

Torry

1. Interview with Tom Raupp.
2. Interview with Bill Saefkow.
3. Interview with Tom Lawton.
4. Interview with Herb Duncan.
5. Interviews with Jim Henderson, Jim Berridge, Patty Barnum Moorhead and Jacqueline Barnum Piallat.
6. Tom Raupp said Roddy was driving no faster than his father, who was at 35 miles per hour.
7. Birmingham Eccentric, January 21, 1965 and the Royal Oak Tribune, January 1965.
8. Interview with Tom Raupp.
9. Interviews with Alex Grether and John Schaeffer.
10. Interview with Harold Jones.
11. Stories swirled through Seaholm the next week that Roddy was conscious and talking. Both Allan Mee, then a student from the east side of Detroit, and Bill Balsley, a classmate of Roddy's, were on the scene. They clearly recall hearing Roddy yelling, "fuck." Other witnesses, however, said Roddy was unconscious and the only sounds came from Mike Adair.
12. Interview with Susan Martin Hyde.
13. Interview with Dick Straight.
14. Interview with Nancy Henderson.
15. Interview with Betty Adair.
16. Interview with Dick Straight.
17. Interview with Betty Adair.
18. Interview with Corey Van Fleet.
19. Interview with Mary Van Fleet.
20. Detroit Free Press, January 18, 1965.
21. Interview with Dr. Robert Pool.
22. Interview with Ellen Adair.
23. Interview with Bob Adams.
24. Interview with Carla Jolly Cleary.
25. Interview with Betsy Brenton Conant.
26. Interview with John Schaeffer.

CHAPTER SEVEN

"I don't think I can swim Friday."

1. Nancy Henderson's diary, January 16, 1965. In 2005, Nancy wrote down additional memories of the night of the accident.
2. Interview with Carla Jolly Cleary.
3. Interview with Krisa Barnum.
4. Nancy Adair's diary, January 16, 1965.
5. Interview with Jim Henderson.
6. Interview with Jacqueline Barnum Piallat.
7. Interview with Chuck Geggie.
8. Interview with Nancy Adair.
9. Interview with Steve Matthews.
10. Interview with Krisa Barnum.
11. Royal Oak Tribune, January 1965.
12. Interview with Kay Hengelmann.
13. Interview with Susan Melcher Pomroy.
14. Interview with Donna Richardson Buchanan.
15. Detroit Free Press, January 19, 1965.
16. Interview with Michael Keener.
17. Detroit Free Press, January 19, 1965.
18. Interview with Ted Blakeslee.
19. Interview with Chuck Geggie.
20. Interview with Susan Berry.
21. Seaholm student newspaper, January 1965.
22. Helen Henderson kept the telegrams in her collection of papers on Roddy.
23. Detroit News, January 18, 1965. The News published on the afternoon of the team meeting.
24. Interview with Corey Van Fleet.
25. Betty Adair relayed to her family the questions Mike asked and Nancy Adair recorded them in her diary, January 18, 1965.
26. Interview with Janice Poplack.

27. Interview with Bob Adams. Years later Bob told his cousin Mike the story of his date.
28. Interview with Susan Melcher Pomroy.
29. Jacquey Barnum Piallat, Patty Barnum Moorhead, Krisa Barnum, Jim Henderson, Nancy Henderson, Donna Bell Zimmer, Sue Melcher Pomroy, Betsy Brenton Conant, Jan Weidner Maraes, Eddie Watkins, Patty Pitcher Parks and Michael Keener provided details of the night at the funeral home. Patty Barnum supplied the list of people who signed the guest book.
30. Interview with Bill Keough.
31. Interview with Betty Adair.
32. Birmingham Eccentric, January 21, 1965.
33. Detroit Free Press, January 19, 1965.
34. Interview with Dorothy Clemens.
35. The letters were published in the Birmingham Eccentric in January and February 1965.
36. Birmingham Eccentric, February 5, 1965.
37. Interview with Mike Adair.
38. Interview with Susan Martin Hyde.
39. In her diary on January 24, 1965, Nancy Adair wrote, "I found out Bruce is becoming conscious now. I'm so glad. He had been in a coma for 8 days."
40. Interview with Mark Morden.
41. Interview with Bruce Berridge.

CHAPTER EIGHT

"Life as we knew it ended that night."

1. Letter from Betty Barnum to Patty Barnum, January 1965. There is no specific date on the letter, but the wording suggests that Betty wrote it on January 25, the second Tuesday after the

accident. Nancy Adair's diary provides additional confirmation. On January 25, 1965, she wrote "the streets were all ice!"

2. Interview with Meredith Martin Cronyn.
3. Letters from Jack Barnum to his father, December 30, 1940, and February 23, 1941.
4. Interview with Krisa Barnum.
5. Interview with Patty Barnum Moorhead.
6. Interview with Patty Barnum Moorhead.
7. Interview with Patty Barnum Moorhead.
8. Nancy Henderson's diary, January 30, 1965.
9. Ibid, February 5, 1965.
10. Ibid, February 13 and February 19, 1965.
11. Ibid, May 25, 1965.
12. Nancy Henderson kept her original copy of the speech.
13. Nancy Henderson's diary, December 14, 1972.
14. Interviews with Jim Henderson and Nancy Henderson.
15. Interview with Jim Henderson.
16. Interview with Dave Nelson.
17. Dick Zemmin's column was published in the Birmingham Eccentric, January 21, 1965.
18. Detroit News, November 16, 1966.
19. Detroit News, January 23, 1966.
20. Birmingham Eccentric, April 28, 1966.
21. In her diary, Nancy Henderson recorded the bands that played at the Teen Center.
22. Interview with Helen Henderson.
23. Letter from Suzanne Pratt to Helen Henderson, March 4, 1965.
24. Interview with Nancy Henderson. She said her mother did not tell her about reading through the letters until 2005.
25. Nancy Henderson's diary, October 2, 1968.
26. Ibid, January 17, 1973 and February 27, 1973.
27. Nancy Henderson's diary, August 15, 1973.
28. Ibid, September 16, 1973.

CHAPTER NINE

"I just came to see Roddy."

1. Detroit Free Press, March 12, 1965.
2. Interviews with Jim Adair and Mike Adair.
3. Interview with Susan Martin Hyde.
4. Betty Adair kept copies of the hospital bills and the letter.
5. Lawsuit filed in Oakland County Circuit Court by the firm of Hartman, Beier, Howlett & McConnell on behalf of the Adair family. In a memorandum, attorney Dean G. Beier suggested "some further investigation be made with regard to the possibility that the driver of the other car was served intoxicants by a licensed alcoholic beverage dispenser."
6. The Adairs and Berridges hired Dean G. Beier of the law firm of Hartman, Beier, Howlett & McConnell of Pontiac, Michigan, which is now the Bloomfield Hills law firm of Beier, Howlett. In his statement of claim, which is on file at the Oakland County Circuit Court, Beier charged that Mike Drothler was negligent because, "(1) he drove at a speed faster than was reasonable under the circumstances and in excess of the speed limit controlling the named public thoroughfare; (2) for no apparent reason, he crossed the center line of West Maple in violation of road markings restricting east boundvehicles to travel on the south side of the thoroughfare, and (3) he drovehis automobile under the influence of intoxicating beverages." In December of 1965, Oakland County Probate Judge Donald E. Adams appointed Pontiac attorney Bernard Girard as the referee "with full power and authority to examine the claims and demands of the claimants." On January 17, 1966, Girard filed his report: "I find the details of the accident as set forth in the 'Statement of Claims' are accurate. This determination is made by the testimony in support of the claims and personal knowledge of the undersigned." On January 27, 1966, Judge Adams issued an order declaring that Girard's report "is hereby adopted as the judgment

and order of this court." Mr. Beier died in 2003, which is before I began work on "Henderson's Light

7. Ibid. and interview with Bob Drothler.
8. Interview with Bill Saefkow.
9.   Interview with Susan Martin Hyde.
10. Interview with Bruce Berridge.
11. Interview with Susan Martin Hyde.
12. Interview with Mike Adair.
13. Interview with Mike Adair.
14. Interview with Betty Adair.
15. Interview with Susan Martin Hyde.
16. Interview with Denton Cooley. Betty Adair recalled the conversation with Larson.
17. Six years later, Dr. Robert Pool, who operated on Mike the night of the accident, saw Cooley and his wife in the lobby of a New York hotel during a medical convention. Pool approached Cooley and said, "I have to congratulate you. That's the best telephone diagnosis I ever heard of. You saved Mike's life." Cooley peppered Pool with questions about Mike. Cooley charged $3,215 for the surgery, while St. Luke's Episcopal Hospital charged $798 for room, lab work and drugs.
18. Interview with Sue Adair Ewing. Although Mike has no recollection of the nightmares, Sue vividly recalls her father telling her about them.
19. Interview with Deborah Harter Williams.
20. Interview with Lesley Swatman Bennett.
21. Interviews with Nancy Ackerly Barton, Sally Splane McWilliams and Susan Melcher Pomroy.
22. Interview with Lesley Swatman Bennett.
23. One of Bruce's best friends told me about the visit to Roddy's grave. Bruce did not recall the night, but conceded during the first couple of years after the accident he often visited his friend's grave.
24. Interviews with Mike Adair and Bruce Berridge.
25. Interview with Dick Lowrie.

26. Interview with Dick Lowrie.
27. Interview with Susan Watkins Adair.
28. Interview with Dave Nelson.
29. Interview with Gina Bugor Berridge.
30. Interviews with Gina Bugor Berridge and Bruce Berridge.
31. Interview with Dick Lowrie.
32. Interviews with Bruce Berridge and Mike Adair.
33. Interview with Susan Watkins Adair.
34. Interviews with Nancy Adair and Sue Adair Ewing.
35. Interview with Bob Pool.

CHAPTER TEN

"Who is Nancy?"

1. Interview with Krisa Barnum.
2. Interview with Krisa Barnum.
3. Interview with Krisa Barnum.
4. Interview with Krisa Barnum.
5. Interview with Krisa Barnum.
6. Interview with Jim Henderson.
7. Nancy Henderson's diary, February 11, 1979.
8. Ibid, August 15, 1979.
9. Ibid, April 16, 1983.
10. Ibid, September 6, 1964 and January 8, 1965.
11. "In Black and White," by Nancy J. Henderson. From "Variations on the Ordinary – A Woman's Reader," edited by Margo LaGattuta, Plain View Press, 1995.
12. Nancy Henderson's diary, April 17, 1983.
13. Nancy Henderson's diary, April 30, 1983.
14. Interview with John Allman.
15. Nancy Henderson's diary, October 26, 1986.
16. Ibid, November 19, 1986.
17. Nancy Henderson's diary, June 21, 1987.

18. Ibid, October 28, 1987.
19. Ibid, March 16, 1988.
20. Ibid, August 24, 1988.
21. Nancy Henderson's diary, April 17, 1992.
22. Ibid, May 6, 1993.
23. "My Brother's Funeral," by Nancy J. Henderson. From "Variations on the Ordinary."
24. "Warming up to Death," by Nancy J. Henderson. From "Variations on the Ordinary."

CHAPTER ELEVEN

"A time to heal"

1. Interview with Mike Adair.
2. Interview with Connie Hydrick Adair.
3. Interview with Connie Hydrick Adair.
4. Interview with Mike Adair.
5. Interview with Susan Melcher Pomroy.
6. Interview with Eddie Watkins.
7. Interview with Nancy Ackerly Barton.
8. Interview with Bruce Berridge.
9. Interview with Gina Bugor Berridge.
10. Interview with Bruce Berridge.
11. Interview with Martha Jean Payton Smith.
12. Interview with Bill Saefkow.
13. Interview with Susan Melcher Pomroy.
14. Interview with Nancy Ackerly Barton.
15. Interview with Susan Melcher Pomroy.

CHAPTER TWELVE

Sunset and Evening Star

1. The Hendersons and Barnums kept copies of the sermon.
2. Interview with Steve Zimmer.
3. Interview with Donna Bell Zimmer.
4. Interview with Anne Le Fevre Haller as well as a letter Anne wrote to Helen Henderson on January 19, 1966.
5. Interview with Nancy Henderson.
6. Interview with Jim Henderson.
7. Interviews with Jacquey Barnum Piallat, Patty Barnum Moorhead and Krisa Barnum.
8. Interview with Betty Adair.

ABOUT THE AUTHOR

Jack Torry covers Congress, the Supreme Court, and politics for the Washington Bureau of the *Columbus Dispatch*. *Henderson's Light* is his second book; his first was *Endless Summers: The Fall and Rise of the Cleveland Indians,* published in 1995 by Diamond Communications. Terry and his wife Saundra live in Leesburg, Virginia.